1993

VOTING AND THE SPIRIT OF AMERICAN DEMOCRACY

VOTING AND THE SPIRIT OF AMERICAN DEMOCRACY

Essays on the History of Voting and Voting Rights in America

Edited by
DONALD W. ROGERS

In Collaboration with Christine Scriabine

UNIVERSITY OF ILLINOIS PRESS
Urbana and Chicago

First published by the University of Illinois Press in 1992
© 1990 by the University of Hartford
Reprinted by arrangement with the copyright holder.

Manufactured in the United States of America
1 2 3 4 5 C P 5 4 3 2 1

This book is printed on acid-free paper.

Library of Congress Cataloging-in-Publication Data

Voting and the spirit of American democracy : essays on the history of
   voting and voting rights in America / edited by Donald W. Rogers in
   collaboration with Christine Scriabine.
       p.   cm.
   Includes bibliographical references.
   ISBN 0-252-01918-0 (cl). — ISBN 0-252-06247-7 (pb)
       1. Suffrage—United States—History. 2. Voting—United States—
   History.   I. Rogers, Donald Wayne.   II. Scriabine, Christine
   Brendel.
   JK1846.V68   1992
   324.6'2'0973—dc20   91-28818
                                                                CIP

The original publication of this book was funded by grants from the National
Endowment for the Humanities and the United States Constitution Bicentennial
Commission of Connecticut.

CONTENTS

ILLUSTRATIONS

ACKNOWLEDGMENTS

T his collection of essays is the product of a public lecture series held at the University of Hartford during the academic year 1988-89 as part of our national bicentennial celebration of the U.S. Constitution. The series received generous funding from the National Endowment for the Humanities under grant GP-21446-88. Senior Grants Officer Wilsonia Cherry and Grants Officer Thomas Phelps were extraordinarily helpful and encouraging in this project. Another generous grant from the U.S. Constitution Bicentennial Commission of Connecticut, along with funds from the NEH grant, paid for preparation and publication of this booklet. The opinions, findings, and conclusions expressed in this volume do not necessarily reflect the views of either organization.

The eight essays in this volume are edited and refined versions of the public lectures. The authors benefitted enormously from remarks and suggestions made by commentators at each lecture. Jack Chatfield, Richard Kay, Richard Buel, William Gienapp, John Sutherland, Robert Kolesar, Barbara Lacey, Anita Mackey, Deborah Calloway, Michael Harris, Teresalee Bertinuson, Christine Scriabine, Regina Dighton, and Walter Markham all tendered thought-provoking remarks at the lectures. Discussions at all of the lectures were uniformly stimulating; members of the audiences deserve much of the credit for making each event interesting, and for enhancing the quality of the essays.

This booklet would not have been possible without terrific institutional support from persons at all levels of the University of Hartford. Senior Vice President for Academic Affairs and Dean of the Faculty Jonathan Lawson furnished resources to hold dinners and public receptions for each of the guest speakers, while Vice President for Academic Administration Richard Whiteside and his staff helped to make scheduling arrangements. Vice President for Public Affairs Belle Ribicoff warmly assisted in working out the logistics for each lecture, and the Development Office's Florence Attas helped to arrange menus and receptions. University of Hartford government grants officer Bonnie Ferrero and accountant Vish Govindasmy furnished essential help in administering the grants properly. Museum of American Political Life Director Edmund Sullivan rendered critical assistance in identifying drawings, buttons, posters and other artifacts to illustrate this volume, while Maryann Bracken and Steve Laschever carefully photographed them. The university's maintenance staff was efficient in setting up lecture rooms, while the food service always provided tasty refreshments at the receptions.

Members of the College of Arts and Sciences participated actively in the lecture series. Strongly supportive was Dean Walter Markham who attended lectures when he could, scraped funds out of the college budget to support the series, and served as commentator at the final lecture. Faculty colleagues Bernard den Ouden and David Dalin also gave warm support, regularly attending and participating in the programs. Jane Edwards, Peter Breit, Chuck Colarulli, Victor D'Lugin, Marcia Moen, Catherine Jones, and Kenneth Minkema also enthusiastically participated. Tamara Moreland of the Career Development and Placement Office was an eager participant.

The History Department provided extraordinary assistance in mastering the logistics of the lecture series, a mastery that prevailed even in the wake of a measles epidemic which nearly forced cancellation of Mary Katzenstein's presentation in March 1989. Department Chair Bill Brayfield's help was vital, as he had the right suggestion to make at every crucial juncture of the series. He attended nearly every lecture, lending support and posing tough questions. Department secretary Carolyn Moore was always available to help, staving off typing crises and tying up loose ends. Special Programs secretary Judy Yoczik and Theater Arts secretary Harriet Baggish also graciously helped with typing. Students Gary Peterson and Jennifer Lewis deserve thanks for courteously greeting guests at each lecture and for distributing programs and questionnaires.

Numerous people and organizations outside the university community were helpful in staging the lectures. Outstanding was the Connecticut Humanities Council's Jane Christie Smith, who offered suggestions for program participants. In addition, Barbara Solow, program chair for the New England Historical Association's 1988 annual meeting, helped to arrange Sean Wilentz's lecture as part of the association's October 1988 program.

Production of this booklet, artistic creation of advertising material, and distribution depended upon the exceptionally skilled University of Hartford Publications Department. SallySue Vimolchalao, Ann Fitzpatrick, Diana Simonds, Nancy Swain, and Richard LeBlanc each played critical roles in various aspects of publicizing the lecture series and producing the booklet. Louis Sampliner and Monika Frey proofread the manuscript in a flawlessly meticulous way, while Rick Walker helped in developing mailing lists.

Absolutely essential to this project, from beginning to end, were two university secretaries, Nancy Lilliquist and Helmi Cotter. They shared in typing the bulk of the correspondence and word processing numerous drafts of the booklet's manuscript. Nancy and Helmi were terrifically dependable and efficient. They were also impressively graceful and cheerful under fire — the fire, that is, of the nervous and anxious editor.

Most important, this whole project would never have happened without the participation of consultant Christine Scriabine of the Museum of American Political Life. Chris developed most of the original grant proposal, and spent countless hours on the telephone lining up speakers. Moreover, she participated in nearly all of the lectures, presenting formal commentary at one. She also devoted considerable energy to reviewing drawings, posters and photographs from the museum's collection to illustrate this booklet, and she offered important editorial suggestions for this booklet's manuscript. Chris was truly a major force behind every phase of this project, and its quality reflects her unfailingly positive influence.

VOTING AND THE SPIRIT OF AMERICAN DEMOCRACY

JAMES MADISON.

Wood engraving by Bono (James Akin), circa 1810, of James Madison, a major figure at the 1787 Philadelphia convention which drafted the U.S. Constitution, and later fourth president of the United States. In a speech at the constitutional convention, Madison defended suffrage as an essential feature of republican government, but he maintained that only property holders should be allowed to vote. *Source: Museum of American Political Life, University of Hartford.*

INTRODUCTION:
THE RIGHT TO VOTE IN AMERICAN HISTORY

Donald W. Rogers
University of Hartford

When Frenchman Alexis de Tocqueville visited the United States in the mid-1830s, he found Americans very enthusiastic about voting. The country was in the midst of a great democratic reform movement that broadened popular participation in the electoral process. Disappearing were the old requirements left over from the colonial years that restricted voting to white male property holders. Emerging were laws which extended the right to vote to virtually all adult white men.

Tocqueville regarded the U.S.'s expansion of voting rights as a reflection of Americans' unique democratic spirit. Because of this spirit, he concluded, Americans had embarked on an unswerving path toward the condition of universal suffrage, in which nearly all adult Americans — black or white, male or female, rich or poor — would have the right to vote. "When a nation begins to modify the elective qualification," he reasoned, "it may easily be foreseen that, sooner or later, that qualification will be entirely abolished." As he explained, "the further that electoral rights are extended, the greater is the need of extending them; for after each concession the strength of democracy increases, and its demands increase with its strength."[1]

The democratic spirit that Tocqueville witnessed in voting rights expansion was seemingly everywhere present in the politics of the mid-1800s. The eligible voters of his day — that is, adult white men — customarily joined political parties, routinely assembled by the thousands in mass political rallies, and regularly paraded to the polls at election time. Most significantly, Americans of Tocqueville's time turned out at the polls in heavy numbers: three out of every four eligible voters regularly cast their ballots throughout most of the nineteenth century. And as Tocqueville predicted, the American democratic spirit helped to bring about the further expansion of voting rights during the next century, first to black men after the Civil War and next to women in 1920.

How times have changed. As we enter the 1990s, voting has become a private act carried out by only a bare majority of the eligible American electorate. Modern voters go to the polls as individuals, rather than parade as members of groups. Little more than 50 percent of eligible voters participate in presidential elections and only a third cast ballots in off-year congressional races. Turnout in state and local races nowadays is usually even lower.

Moreover, compared to nineteenth-century voters' enthusiasm for electioneering, modern Americans seem to be demoralized about the electoral process. They complain that the calibre of campaign debate is depressingly low, that candidates are lackluster and do not inspire voters to vote, and most importantly, that their votes "do not make a difference." Government is no longer accessible to the average citizen, modern Americans say: it has become a remote bureaucracy more responsive to rich people, big business, and organized interests such as PACs (political action committees) than to the average voter.

The decline of voter participation and the corresponding demoralization of modern-day voters constitute one of the most significant developments of twentieth-century politics. If the essence of political democracy rests in the citizenry's ability to select its own leaders through universal suffrage, then it is a startling fact that a larger and larger proportion of the contemporary American electorate declines to go to the polls. If half of our eligible voters do not vote, whom does our government really represent? Do modern voting trends reflect a democracy in decay, the decline of our representative system of government?

This booklet addresses these questions by placing the problem of voting in the context of our country's 380-year history. The booklet consists of eight essays by distinguished historians and political scientists who examine crucial phases of the historical development of voting and voting rights from the founding of the British North American colonies down to the present day. The value of looking at voting historically rests not only in seeing "how we came to be the way we are today" or in evaluating "how far we have progressed" toward achieving democratic ideals. The historical perspective can also help us to understand how changing social circumstances affected the workings of our political system, particularly the right to vote.

American society has experienced radical changes in its 380-year history. It evolved from an agrarian to urban-industrial nation. It populated much of North America with immigrants from Europe, Africa and Asia. It established and later expunged the institution of African slavery, laying the groundwork for our modern concern with the civil rights of minorities and women. It erected a welfare state to contend with the modern problems of unemployment, old age and poverty. And it created the technological base for today's mass-media oriented consumer society. All of these developments drastically altered the social context in which the representative features of our government operated. The evolving social context has produced important changes in both the meaning of politics and the meaning of the right to vote.

From the very early years of our history, one of the unchanging bedrocks of our political culture has been the principle of "popular sovereignty" — that is, rule by the people. This principle is captured in the opening words of the U.S. Constitution: "We the People . . . do ordain and establish this Constitution for the United States of America." According to this principle, American government is to be the creature of the sovereign people, and its purpose is to serve the people's will faithfully, as the people periodically express it in elections. As historian Edmund S. Morgan has explained, "In elections the fiction of popular sovereignty makes its strongest approach to reality, as actual people ostensibly go about selecting from among themselves the few" who will represent them in government.[2] Elections actively demonstrate that American government is — at least, theoretically — an extension of the people's will.

But who are "the People"? And under what circumstances can "the People" be confident that elections reflect their will and make government responsible to it? The essays in this volume make clear that although American government was founded on the practice of frequent elections, enormous amounts of political energy throughout American history have been expended on deciding which Americans can vote on behalf of "the People" and on organizing electoral machinery so that the voice of voters can be heard.

Throughout American history, the most important political struggles concerning voting have pertained to "suffrage rights" or "the franchise" — that is, the legal definition of who is eligible to cast ballots. In the beginning, suffrage laws extended the right to vote primarily to white male landowners, not to all adult American citizens. As Alexis de Tocqueville found out, however, American politics has democratic tendencies. These tendencies led to the broadening of suffrage rights throughout the nineteenth and twentieth centuries, until today, when nearly all adult citizens eighteen years of age and above are included in the "electorate," the total pool of eligible voters.

The struggle to define the electorate, however, has not always been democratically inclined. Toward the end of the nineteenth century, reformers introduced changes in registration requirements and electoral procedures which were designed to restrict the exercise of suffrage rights only to "competent" voters. The effect was to exclude southern blacks from the electoral process, and to discourage poor, urban voters in the North and Midwest from going to the polls.

Not only have debates over the extension of suffrage defined who "the People" are, but so also has the behavior of voters themselves. Throughout American history, the *actual* electorate has often differed from the total *eligible* electorate. Despite laws which give them the right to vote, eligible voters for one reason or another do not always choose to exercise that right. Indeed, low voter "turnout" or "participation" has been a major problem at various stages of American history. It may surprise the modern reader to know that turnout rates during the colonial period were just as low as they are today, making the actual colonial electorate only a tiny fraction of the whole American population. A mere 6 percent of the American population elected George Washington as our first president!

Another problem, increasingly significant since the 1950s, has been the political efficacy of voting. How much does every vote really count? Does every vote have a political impact? Lawsuits in federal courts during the 1950s and 1960s challenged "malapportioned" election districts — that is, districts that awarded some voters greater political representation than others. The problem arose as a result of population shifts from rural to urban areas. Because state legislatures failed to redraw district lines, rural voters gradually received proportionally more representatives than urban voters in Congress and state assemblies. In response to lawsuits filed against this practice, the U.S. Supreme Court established the legal doctrine of "one man, one vote," reaffirming the requirement that state legislatures periodically reapportion election districts in a way that every ballot — rural or urban — was counted equally in electing representatives.

The Civil Rights Movement of the 1950s and 1960s produced another kind of court challenge relating to voting's efficacy. Lawsuits filed under the provisions of the 1965 Voting Rights Act challenged electoral procedures, common in the South, in which county and municipal officials were elected in at-large elections or in multi-member districts. According to civil rights activists, these procedures deprived minority voters of a "meaningful ballot," because they prevented minority voters from placing any of their own candidates in office.

Suffrage rights, voter turnout, and voting's political efficacy are the principal subjects of the essays in this volume. The central theme of this collection, however, is *historical change*. Although we tend to think of voting in the context of the ideal of popular democracy — that is, a broadly-based citizenry actively engaged in the electoral process — the essays in this volume demonstrate that both the practice and the meaning of voting have changed a great deal. As a result of social, economic and political changes throughout our nation's 380-year history, voting has evolved through three stages of development.

The first stage spanned the seventeenth and eighteenth centuries, when the British North American colonies were founded and when the United States was established as the world's first modern republic. From the very beginning, government in the colonies rested partly on a popular base. Whether created by joint stock company, royal charter, or proprietary fiat, colonial governments incorporated representative assemblies into their structures.

During the early-eighteenth century, American colonists came to view the structure of their governments in the context of the British theory of "mixed government," or government whose branches perfectly balanced the three basic elements of society — monarchy, aristocracy, and the people. Just as the British constitutional system featured the Crown, the House of Lords, and the House of Commons, colonial governments typically consisted of a governor appointed by the King, a council appointed by the governor or chosen by the assembly, and a popularly elected assembly. In both Great Britain and America, the popular branch was deemed crucial to preserving both liberty and order, as it counteracted royal authority and limited aristocratic power. Voting, then, was central to the maintenance of well-ordered government.

The colonial electorate was much different than it is today. Actual voters constituted only a tiny proportion of the total population, and voting was generally restricted to the "better" elements of society. As Christopher Collier explains in this volume's first essay, "The American People as Christian White Men of Property," voting during the colonial years was restricted by both legal and nonlegal factors. First of all, colonial laws defined eligibility on the basis of property-holding, generally a "freehold" of land. By law, blacks, women and some non-Protestants were not eligible to vote. In addition, the agrarian nature of colonial society curtailed voting, as the difficulty of travelling over rough roads kept some voters from the polls. Extremely important also was the political custom of "deference," where potential voters of the middling and lower social orders deferred to the authority of their social betters. Though colonial officeholders were expected to pay close attention to the wishes of their constituents, voting and officeholding were dominated by the social elite that presumably could best represent the common good. As observers of the time often remarked, colonial politics consisted of "a speaking aristocracy in the face of a silent majority."

Political philosophy during the colonial era supported rule by the elite. Based on the intellectual tradition of civic humanism, a tradition which dominated Western European nations and the American colonies during most of the seventeenth and eighteenth centuries, colonial political life stressed public service and devotion to the common good. In this context, voting and officeholding were acts of civic duty which the social elite were obliged to do on behalf of the commonweal. Colonists thought that the social elite were well prepared to discern the common good and were obligated to protect it.

The period of the American Revolution — 1760s, 1770s, and 1780s — brought an end to the reign of civic humanism and the colonial pattern of voting. The imperial clashes between Great Britain and the colonies that culminated in the American Revolution inspired colonists to rethink the meaning of politics and voting's place in it.

British taxes in the 1760s and 1770s — most notoriously the Stamp Act of 1765 and the Tea Tax of 1773 — provided the spark for the American War for Independence. More important for the American political development, however, were diverging conceptions of voting on the two sides of the Atlantic Ocean. It was conventional wisdom in eighteenth-century England that the House of Commons, the popular branch, *virtually* represented all of the people, because members of the Commons shared interests similar to those of the people at large. Thus, according to English theory, even *colonists* enjoyed Parliamentary representation, although not a single colonist sat in the House of Commons.

After a century of experience with local rule through their colonial assemblies, however, colonists argued that the people deserved *actual* representation in government, particularly when money questions were involved. Not only should delegates to assemblies represent local viewpoints, colonists held, but also they should be elected from among their own constituents. Colonial assemblies, in the words of Boston lawyer and future President of the United States John Adams, "should think, feel, reason, and act like" the people who elected them.[3] So keen were colonists about having their elected officials faithfully represent their wishes, that they commonly imposed residency requirements and even issued written instructions to keep delegates in touch with constituents. Given the colonial preference for faithful, actual representation, is it any surprise that the cry of "taxation without representation" rang out when Parliament passed the Tea Act in 1773 without direct colonial consent?

By the time of the American Revolution, then, American colonists regarded the popular branch of government, their elected assemblies, as the repository of their rights and liberties as English people. Colonists' faith in the popular branch soon turned into constitutional principle. By the end of the 1780s, when the Philadelphia convention framed the U.S. Constitution, Americans had abandoned the idea of mixed government — that is, government based on the balance of monarchy, aristocracy, and the people — and they invented the idea of "republicanism," a system of government resting on the consent of the people alone. In the new scheme of things, the people established the federal government through popularly elected ratifying conventions, and they held the federal government accountable through the practice of periodic elections for president, vice president, and Congress.

During the half-century following the American Revolution, a gradual democratization of politics ushered in the second stage of suffrage development, a stage that spanned most of the nineteenth century. This new era was characterized by the breakdown of the deferential style of politics, the emergence of egalitarian politics, the gradual opening of the political process to the average citizen, and most importantly, the gradual expansion of suffrage rights.

A major shift in political philosophy reinforced these trends. Civic humanism gradually gave way to the Liberal tradition, the system of political values that still prevails in the United States today. While civic humanism stressed the interest of the community as a whole, the Liberal tradition emphasized the rights of individuals, particularly in property, political expression and personal liberty. Under the Liberal tradition, Americans still considered voting as a civic duty, but they came to see voting more as a political right that enabled individuals to "protect their interests."

The central vehicle for the democratization of nineteenth-century politics was the political party, which first appeared during the 1790s and emerged in something resembling its modern form after Andrew Jackson's election as president in 1828. Jackson's presidency spawned the development of a competitive national political party system, in which two major parties (the Democrats and the Whigs) contended for power. The partisan competition of the Jacksonian years started the era of what historian Michael McGerr calls "popular politics," an era in which political parties' basic function was to mobilize thousands of Americans, rich and poor (though still exclusively white and male), and bring them directly into contact with the political process. Popular politics was a central thread of nineteenth-century American life. Party allegiance shaped Americans' social consciousness, and party activities — such as spectacular campaigning, complete with uniformed marching units and torchlight parades — engaged nearly every white American man in politics.[4]

One of the major products of popular politics was the rapid expansion of the electorate. Because the principal aim of nineteenth-century political parties was to win elections by mobilizing voters, parties sought to expand (and in a few cases contract) the pool of eligible voters, mainly by eliminating legal barriers to voting. During the 1810s, 1820s, and 1830s, political parties often campaigned on the promise of eliminating property requirements for voting. Then, following the Civil War, the Republican party sponsored the Fifteenth Amendment to the U.S. Constitution, which banned voting restrictions based on race, partly in the hope that thousands of ex-slaves would be converted into voters for the Republican party.

This progressive widening of suffrage rights emanated not only from party activity, but also from fundamental social changes that transformed nineteenth-century America. Colonial property-holding requirements for voting were tied, as Christopher Collier argues in the first essay, to the agrarian character of colonial America. In a society made up almost exclusively of small farmers, the typical voter was a white, Protestant, male landowner. But with the coming of the early-nineteenth-century commercial revolution, Sean Wilentz maintains in his essay, "Property and Power," a nonlandholding producer class developed, leading to social pressures to widen the suffrage. As a result, social class (as defined by property ownership) was virtually eliminated as a criterion for determining voting rights.

An additional social change which affected voting rights during the early-nineteenth century was the influx of European immigrants. During the 1840s and 1850s, more than two million Irish Catholics arrived in America. Different in religion, culture, and social class from the middle-class Protestant American majority, these immigrants confronted efforts from native-born Americans to restrict their political rights. As Paul Kleppner maintains in his essay, "Defining Citizenship," nativist (that is, native-born Americans of English stock) politicians tried to blunt immigrants' political influence by lengthening residency requirements needed to secure naturalized citizenship status. Had their program been successful, nativists would have delayed the day when each immigrant could cast his first ballot. But partisan competition protected immigrants' voting rights by preventing the nativist plan from ever being enacted into law.

The political battles of the 1840s and 1850s over immigrants' naturalization status prefigured an important development in the history of suffrage. The right to vote was increasingly linked to the rights of American citizenship. This development was confirmed in the post-Civil War amendments to the Constitution. Not only did the Civil War bring about the end of American Negro slavery (with the Thirteenth Amendment), and begin the process of incorporating African-Americans into the political mainstream by declaring them citizens (the Fourteenth Amendment), and protecting black men's right to vote (the Fifteenth Amendment), the Civil War also introduced two new concepts into constitutional law: the principles of national citizenship and equal protection before the law.

As Eric Foner maintains in his essay, "From Slavery to Citizenship," these two constitutional principles revolutionized the legal status of black Americans. Before the Civil War, he notes, state laws prohibited black voting, and even the U.S. Constitution protected slavery. The Fourteenth and Fifteenth Amendments, however, put black men on an equal legal footing with whites for the first time, and promised to incorporate them into the political system.

Moreover, the idea of national citizenship rights was the inspiration for the post-Civil War movement on behalf of women's voting rights. Assuming that they had the legal right to vote by virtue of their claim to citizenship, Ellen Carol DuBois argues in her essay, "Taking Law into Their Own Hands," women went to polling places during the early-1870s demanding to cast their ballots. Some male poll watchers allowed them to do so, while others did not. Ultimately, the U.S. Supreme Court denied that voting was a privilege of citizenship in 1875, and it was not until 1920, when the Nineteenth or Women's Suffrage Amendment was ratified, that women's voting rights were finally constitutionally secured.

Ratification of the Fifteenth Amendment in 1870 and the Nineteenth Amendment in 1920 marked major changes in the constitutional status of voting rights. The two amendments barred states or the federal government from denying or abridging voting rights on the basis of race or sex. In terms of the black-letter law, at least, African-Americans and women were incorporated into the electoral system. With the ratification of the Twenty-Sixth Amendment in 1971, American law extended voting rights to eighteen-year-olds as well. By the end of the twentieth century, hence, voting rights expansion had made the American political system one of the most open in the world.

At the same time that the women's suffrage campaign reached its successful conclusion during the first two decades of the twentieth century, the democratic period of American suffrage history ended and the third phase began. This final phase, running roughly from the late-1890s to today, has been characterized by two seemingly contradictory trends: a broad-based decline in voter participation and the simultaneous growth in the efforts of certain blocs of voters to secure a "meaningful ballot," that is, real power in the electoral process.

In the presidential election of 1876, American voter participation reached a historic high of 81.8 percent, and through the 1880s and 1890s, it averaged nearly 80 percent. But during the decades that followed, turnout gradually dwindled until it bottomed out at a level of 48.9 percent in 1924. The creation of the Democratic party's "New Deal Coalition" during the Great Depression of the 1930s somewhat revived voter interest, as turnout grew to around 60 percent, but turnout began to decline again in 1968, plummeting to a low of 50.2 percent in the presidential election of 1988.

While commentators are not wholly sure why turnout has declined, the disappearance of mass partisan activity toward the end of the nineteenth century seems to be a major factor. Led by the Republicans in the 1880s and 1890s, the two major political parties began turning to organized financial support, rather than to a mass political base, to win elections. The campaign chest replaced the torchlight parade.

Moreover, as popular politics came increasingly to be associated with immigrants, the urban working class, and machine politics in the North, and with the black-supported Populist party in the South, partisan electoral activity was discredited among middle-class reformers. To eliminate what they regarded as "corrupt" electoral practices, reformers introduced legislation which changed electoral machinery. In the South, "Jim Crow" laws disfranchised blacks through such devices as the poll tax, literacy tests and the grandfather clause. In the North, complicated registration procedures prevented abuses in urban politics, and at the same time, established the bureaucratic hurdles that discourage minority and poor voters from voting today.

At the same time that partisanship waned and election laws created barriers to voting, special interest groups developed to influence government through collective action. Some were organized as legislative lobbies or pressure groups, but others took the form of voting blocs led by entrepreneurial political figures who identified themselves as leaders of specific groups, such as ethnic voters, racial minorities, and women. One of the central political aims of these voting blocs in the twentieth century has been to translate their votes into favorable government action regarding their constituencies' special needs.

Has bloc voting been effective? Has it given self-conscious political constituencies such as women and racial minorities political representation as groups? Leaders of the women's suffrage movement hoped that ratification of the Nineteenth Amendment in 1920 would give women a clear voice in the political process. In spite of the establishment of the League of Women Voters in the 1920s to inform women about political issues, however, women did not emerge as a unified voting bloc. Nor did they rally behind a single political organization, such as the National Women's Party. Indeed, the new women voters of the 1920s mirrored the complex and diversified political behavior of men.

Nonetheless, as Mary Fainsod Katzenstein contends in her essay, "Constitutional Politics and the Feminist Movement," the political mobilization that women experienced in their campaign to secure ratification of the women's suffrage amendment irrevocably changed their role in political life. Confined to home and largely excluded from politics until the early years of the twentieth century, women broke an important social barrier when they officially cast their first ballots in the presidential election of 1920. This breakthrough paved the way for other activities in the public sphere, especially in social reform, according to Katzenstein. And just as the suffrage campaign enlarged women's role in political life in the 1920s, Katzenstein submits, so did the unsuccessful 1970s campaign for an Equal Rights Amendment lay the groundwork for women's activism in the 1980s.

The fruits of constitutional change were not nearly as immediate for black Americans. While the Fifteenth Amendment protected black men's right to vote, the amendment's success depended upon the supportive political climate of the post-Civil War era, a climate that dissipated through the final decades of the 1800s. As white northern voters turned their attention to industrial development in the 1870s, they lost interest in supporting the continued federal military presence in the reconstructed South that was necessary to enforce black political rights. After federal troops were withdrawn in the late-1870s, white southern Democrats systematically undercut black voting rights, virtually excluding blacks from southern politics during the first half of the twentieth century.

According to Linda Faye Williams in her essay, "The Civil Rights Movement: The Quest for a More Perfect Union," it was not until blacks themselves mobilized in the Civil Rights Movement of the 1950s and 1960s that federal protection for black votes was once again restored. One of the crowning achievements of the Civil Rights Movement, she says, was the 1965 Voting Rights Act providing for federal enforcement of black voting rights in the South.

That blacks secured voting rights protections, however, did not ensure their influence in the political system. While federal voting rights protections have substantially increased the number of black elected officials and increased black voting participation, Williams points out, blacks still have major barriers to hurdle. One barrier consists of southern electoral practices, such as the multi-member district, which bar black candidates from office. Another barrier is the difficulty of translating black votes into needed government action against the problems of unemployment and poverty that plague black America. The quest for a "meaningful ballot," Williams concludes, is black voters' main problem.

Ironically, while leaders of special groups of voters, such as black Americans, have endeavored to improve their constituents' access to the ballot, the overall level of electoral participation has declined during the twentieth century. Although voter turnout in presidential elections exceeded 60 percent during the 1950s, it has gradually declined since then. And the decline has taken place not only among disadvantaged groups, but also among those groups rated by political scientists as most likely to vote: the well-educated, affluent, white middle class.

Not only has voter turnout declined, but also there has been marked change in voters' political attitudes, at least compared to that of the popular style of the nineteenth century. The modern voter is not as likely to get as personally involved in political campaigns as his nineteenth-century counterpart: he or she is more likely to watch thirty-second political advertisements on television than to attend a political rally. Moreover, while most modern voters have partisan affiliations, they are less committed to their party's success than to the success of individual candidates. Finally, modern voters have less confidence than their nineteenth-century predecessors that their votes make a difference. Political scientists have noted a growing level of alienation among voters based largely on the feeling of powerlessness — many voters report feeling that "I don't matter."[5]

The growing level of voter alienation and the long-term decline in voter participation in the twentieth century have left many observers worrying about the state of the American political process. Is American democracy failing? In the final essay in this volume, "Participation in American Elections," Everett Carll Ladd contends that low voter turnout is not necessarily a sign of either a declining democratic spirit among the American people or a failure of representative government. The level of nonvoting, he asserts, is not really that much lower than that in other democratic countries today, despite electoral statistics often cited in newspapers. More important, nonvoting has not, so far, left important segments of the American population without a voice in government. On balance, Ladd contends, nonvoters have the same political attitudes as voters. American government, he concludes, is still effective as a representative political system.

If nonvoting does not signal the failure of our democratic system, however, it does illuminate a central irony in the American political experience. Since the American Revolution, the ideal of popular democracy has seemingly guided American politics toward being the most open political system in the world, especially with the extension of suffrage rights to nearly all adult Americans eighteen years old and above. Nonetheless, in recent times, growing ranks of eligible voters have increasingly declined to go to the polls.

The popular reaction to the growing level of nonvoting is to blame the American voter. Modern commentators complain about voters' complacency — a flagging commitment to live up to their civic duty to vote. Other observers warn about the growing alienation of modern voters — the feeling that in modern bureaucratic America voting does not matter.

The essays in this volume demonstrate, however, that the reasons for nonvoting are more subtle than popular explanations. Contemporary nonvoting is deeply rooted in social and historical developments. The changing social environment of the twentieth century has heavily affected both voters' attitudes and voters' behavior. With the demise of the popular style of politics that boosted partisan activity during the mid-1800s and the rise of modern bureaucratic government, the social circumstances that once supported a high level of voter turnout no longer exist today. Indeed, high voter turnout during the 1800s ought not to be seen simply as evidence of strong democratic zeal among nineteenth-century American voters, but more importantly as a reflection of unique social and political conditions that have not been duplicated in the twentieth century.

Nonetheless, it does seem that modern Americans have lost some democratic zeal compared to the vibrant spirit of the mid-1800s. Although they may still believe in the ideal of popular democracy, Americans behave in a manner surprisingly reminiscent of their eighteenth-century ancestors. Suffrage rights have been vastly expanded compared to the laws of the colonial period, but a large proportion of the modern electorate defers to an elite to do its political work. Like the middling colonists who deferred to the leadership of the merchant and planter elite, the modern voter defers to the bureaucrats who run business, government, and even political parties. If the United States is truly to remain a government of "the People," modern voters might take a lesson from the democratic spirit of nineteenth-century voters. They must "take the law into their own hands" by mobilizing in mass to go out and vote.

NOTES

1. *Democracy in America* (New York, 1945), I: 59.

2. Edmund S. Morgan, *Inventing the People: The Rise of Popular Sovereignty in England and America* (New York, 1988), 174.

3. Ibid., 241.

4. See Michael E. McGerr, *The Decline of Popular Politics: The American North, 1865-1928* (New York, 1986), 3-41.

5. Ruy A. Teixeira, *Why Americans Don't Vote: Turnout Decline in the United States, 1964-1984* (Westport, Ct., 1987), 11-20.

SUGGESTED READINGS

Burnham, Walter Dean. *The Current Crisis in American Politics.* New York: Oxford University Press, 1982.

McGerr, Michael E. *The Decline of Popular Politics: The American North, 1865-1928.* New York: Oxford University Press, 1986.

Morgan, Edmund S. *Inventing the People: The Rise of Popular Sovereignty in England and America.* New York: W. W. Norton & Company, 1988.

Piven, Frances Fox and Richard A. Cloward. *Why Americans Don't Vote.* New York: Pantheon Books, 1988.

Teixeira, Ruy A. *Why Americans Don't Vote: Turnout Decline in the United States.* Westport, Ct.: Greenwood Press, 1987.

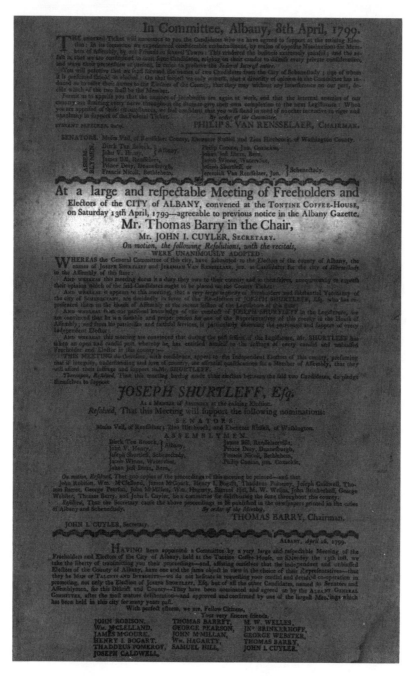

Broadside, April 1799, announcing a meeting of "freeholders" from Albany, New York, to select candidates for the New York state legislature. At the time, only owners of a "freehold" of land were eligible to vote, and so the typical late-eighteenth-century voter was a "respectable" Protestant, white, male landholder. *Source: Museum of American Political Life, University of Hartford.*

1 THE AMERICAN PEOPLE AS CHRISTIAN WHITE MEN OF PROPERTY: SUFFRAGE AND ELECTIONS IN COLONIAL AND EARLY NATIONAL AMERICA

Christopher Collier
University of Connecticut

In modern-day America, observers bemoan the low proportion of eligible voters who turn out to vote at elections. Yet, during the colonial period of American history, an even smaller proportion of the total population participated in elections than today. This may seem surprising, since popular selection of colonial assemblies, as well as of county and village officials, became a regular feature of colonial governance as early as the 1640s. Yet, the combination of British political customs and the overwhelmingly agrarian character of colonial America erected important legal, social, and psychological barriers to voting.

British settlement of North America lasted more than a century, with the first permanent colony planted in Jamestown in 1607 and the last established in Georgia in 1733. The vast majority of colonists were white, Protestant descendants of British citizens, although there were a sizeable number of Scots-Irish, French and German immigrants, and of course, a growing number of enslaved Africans. By the time of the American Revolution in 1776, there were thirteen British colonies stretching a thousand miles along the Atlantic coast and penetrating the continent by several hundred miles. Although there were the makings of a colonial elite — the southern planter class and a northern merchant class — the vast majority of Americans lived on small, self-sufficient farms or in small farming villages. Landholding was widespread, but the elite still retained social authority. It was out of this social setting that the colonial electorate evolved. In the following essay, Christopher Collier examines the composition of that electorate in an effort to explain why it represented such a small proportion of the total colonial population.

Voting and American Democracy

I t is generally reported by scholars who have looked into the matter, that about 6 percent of the total United States population voted for the presidential electors who chose George Washington in 1789.[1] That was a much smaller number of voters than usually turned out for the colony and local elections during most of the eighteenth century. Scholars agree that from 50 to 80 percent of the adult white males were eligible to vote in the colonial period. Since white adult males made up about 20 percent of the population, we have figures of 10 to 16 percent of the *whole population* who might be eligible to vote by the eve of the Revolution.[2] Our best estimates for *actual* voters among adult white males run from about 40 percent in Virginia down to 25 percent or even 10 percent in Massachusetts and Connecticut.[3]

The size of the colonial electorate might seem small, in light of the dramatic expansion of suffrage that has taken place since the American Revolution. Eligibility and participation increased throughout the nineteenth century with the removal of property and religious qualifications completed by the 1840s, and with the removal of race as a qualification by the Fifteenth Amendment to the U.S. Constitution in 1870. The Nineteenth Amendment (1920) prohibited states from discriminating against women in the elective franchise, and in our own day minors between the age of eighteen and twenty-one have been similarly protected by the Twenty-Sixth Amendment (1971).[4] Thus today we would expect a vastly enlarged proportion of the total population to show up at the polls on election day.

But taking into account presidential elections only — those which today call forth the largest number of voters — what do we find? Late-nineteenth-century reformers attempted to undercut urban machine bosses and the old planter aristocracy in the South by establishing registration systems which deprived each group of supposedly "corrupt" elements of its voter base. This meant disfranchising immigrants and the uneducated in the North and blacks in the South. Voter registration — dating for the most part only from the 1890s and the first quarter of the twentieth century — drastically reduced the number of eligibles.

Such regulations continue to eliminate very large numbers of potential voters from the polls today. Nearly one-third of voting-age Americans were not registered in 1988, and only about 50 percent of those registered actually voted. Americans over eighteen years of age constituted just about 70 percent of the population in 1988. About 46 percent of the population was registered to vote, and 50 percent of those registered actually voted — or about 23 percent of the total population voted for president in 1988.[5] Thus the percent of *eligible voters* who did vote in 1988 is no greater, and probably a good deal less, than it was during the colonial period. But the percent of the *total population* now voting is roughly seven times what it was in Washington's first election, or perhaps four times what it might have been in hotly contested colonial elections or in 1836, when for the first time all states provided for popular selection of presidential electors. With the contemporary scene in mind, let me sketch the picture as it appeared in the colonial era.

The most recent general survey of colonial elections, published in 1977, tells us that between 10 and 40 percent of the adult white males turned out to vote in elections in the eighteenth century before the American Revolution. (It hazards no guess at all about the seventeenth century.) But variation among colonies was considerable. Elections in Virginia saw as much as 57 percent on one occasion, but usually hovered around 40 percent. At the other end of the scale, elections for colony-wide officers in Connecticut rarely brought out more than 20 percent of the adult white males, and figures closer to 10 percent were more common. Calculations for all the colonies are based on very few returns, and in any event have to be sharply qualified by a number of significant conditions.[6]

In the first place, not all adult white males were eligible to vote. If we alter our figures to relate actual voters to eligible voters (rather than to the total number of adult males), our percentages might double, even more in the case of Connecticut, and increase by as much as 25 percent in Virginia. A second major qualification is that in some colonies, a two-tier system of elections — with more property required for voting for higher offices — separated local contests from colony-wide contests, and voters expressed much greater concern for local issues and officers than colony-wide elections. This was distinctly the case in Connecticut, where one well-informed observer declared that three times as many men voted in local elections as in colony elections.[7] This is, of course, the reverse of the contemporary situation where presidential elections bring out many more voters than do local and state contests.

Another factor limiting the number of men who turned out to vote in the colonial period was the attitude of social deference, the acceptance of a hierarchical society which was divided between the better sort, the middling sort, and the lower orders. The last of these were not eligible to vote, and the middling tended to let neighbor George do the voting when George was wealthy or enjoyed some other evidence of accomplishment or status. Those who came to the polls voted for their betters, and since so many elections were virtually uncontested, or contested by two rich peas in a pod, there was little motivation to take the time or make the effort to travel to the polls. There may have been an element of apathy or cynicism in this deference, but whatever it was, it tended to keep men home on election day.[8]

A fourth consideration is distance. Polling places were often a day's travel away — sometimes two days and even more. Time away from the farm was not undertaken lightly in the agricultural economy of the colonial years. And the expense of lodging at an inn for a night or two merely to vote in frequently preordained elections was not money well spent or justifiable to wives who so often held the purse strings. The problem of distance certainly underlay what many historians usually attribute to apathy, complacency, cynicism and deference. How many Americans today would make a strenuous effort — say a one- or two-day round trip in an automobile — to vote in even a closely contested election?

Deference, distance, and a detached view of colony as opposed to local elections all took their toll on voter turnout. But the most significant single factor holding down the number of voters was the eligibility requirements established in every colony — limiting voters invariably to adult white males. To begin with, that group constituted only about 20 percent of the colonial population, a markedly more youthful one than that of today. Except in the very earliest years of colonial settlement, when men as young as seventeen voted in some elections, and for a brief period when Massachusetts set the age at twenty-four, all the colonies established twenty-one as the minimum age of eligibility for voting. This is not hard for most of us to accept, since the Twenty-Sixth Amendment has been on the books only since 1971, and since the twenty-one-year-old criterion was rooted in ancient English tradition. Indeed, for many of us today, it is the eighteen-year rather than the twenty-one-year limit that is hard to accept. So much for the adult part of the triad of colonial qualifications. What about the male part?

The question of sexual inequality was one that never even came up in the context of voting rights in the colonial era. Apparently there were cases of women voting in elections — women who had inherited their husbands' property and business. But they were extremely rare and were considered at the time to be freakish. Women did not vote, could not be voters, could not hold office and only very, very rarely participated in politics at all.[9] As late as the late-nineteenth century it was believed by many — that is, many *men* — that contemplation of matters political — as with contemplation of any abstract field such as mathematics — would overtax the female intelligence and drive the adventuresome lady into the insane asylum.

Women and children could not vote. And neither, for the most part could the propertyless. In all colonies men had to own property in order to qualify for the suffrage. The reasons for this are simple enough to understand. Since government was established to protect property and personal freedom, those who controlled the government ought to possess some of each.[10] The idea that only property holders should be allowed to vote grew out of what is called the stake-in-society theory — one's stake in society was measured by how much of its tangible elements one owned. This, of course, was related largely to the question of taxation. Men without property in most cases would pay little or no taxes and therefore should not be in a position to influence the amount of taxes to be paid. Secondly, the possession of property in the preindustrial, prewage and largely non-cash economy provided economic and therefore political independence. If you were beholden to no landlord or no wage-paying employer, or no creditor, then you were free to vote your own interests or your own conscience or your own sense of the public good. No one could extort your vote or influence you by economic leverage.[11] Property, in other words, provided not only economic independence, but political independence as well.

Specific property requirements for the suffrage franchise in colonial America differed from place to place, but that most widely used was the forty pound freehold, an English tradition since the fourteenth century. Under this provision, potential voters had to own property — usually real estate — that was worth forty pounds, or that returned forty shillings a year (that's a 5 percent return) in rent or interest. In some colonies, the requirement could be fulfilled with personal property, which in most cases meant livestock. Many colonies also assessed each adult male a poll — that is, evaluated him at some worth and then taxed him on it. In some cases that poll could also be counted towards the forty pounds. As the seventeenth and eighteenth centuries waned, however, and colonial paper money began to circulate, monetary inflation followed, and the forty pounds became increasingly easy to accumulate. As a result, some colonies began stating the freehold qualification in numbers of acres held, rather than its value in pounds. One hundred acres was common, but over time, fifty acres became a more likely standard.

Historians have debated very strenuously the affect of these property requirements on limiting the suffrage. In the early-twentieth century, assertions were made — and widely accepted — that these qualifications restricted voting rights to a very small number, giving colonial politics a highly aristocratic character. These views came under attack beginning in the 1950s. Incremental findings over the years have produced the modern view that by the eve of the Revolution, property requirements did little to limit the number of eligible voters. Indeed, several studies show that voting — at least on the local level — was quite promiscuous in that legal requirements were often ignored and that just about anybody who looked like a voter was permitted to vote if he wanted to.[12]

In addition to age, sex, and property requirements, many colonies insisted upon terms of residency for voters. The most common was one year, though Georgia and North Carolina called for six months only, while Pennsylvania and Delaware made it two years. These are all the more notable because there was no such tradition in England. But in the colonies, with their high immigration rates, there was considerable concern about non-English speaking residents who lacked knowledge of local institutions, traditions, and issues. Much anti-German rhetoric was expended not only in New York, but also in Pennsylvania, where Benjamin Franklin was a particularly vehement polemicist against the third of the colony's mid-eighteenth-century population that spoke German. No colony, however, actually established either a literacy or an English language requirement for the suffrage, in the expectation, presumably, that a term of residency would acquaint potential voters with the local situation.

None of these requirements seem bizarre to the modern American, for whom even the disqualification of women is a familiar historical fact. But less easy to assimilate is the idea that all the colonies restricted voting to Protestant Christians. In some places the franchise was limited even to certain Protestant sects, as in Massachusetts where for most of the seventeenth century only Congregationalists could vote. In the southern states where the Anglican church was established — that is, the official, tax-supported church — Quakers, Baptists, and Presbyterians were barred from the polling places. Legislation against Catholic suffrage was passed in Virginia in 1699, and several other colonies followed that example. Even Rhode Island, with its vaunted religious freedom, forbade Catholics from voting by legislation enacted in 1719. That colony also excluded Jews from the suffrage franchise as did, at one time or another during the colonial period, six other colonies.

In my trilogy of basic eligibility requirements, I have included the word white largely as a matter of convention. Few colonies legislated American Indians or Negroes out of the suffrage. Such legislation dates from the early-nineteenth century. Nevertheless, no instances of blacks or Indians voting have been discovered in the northern colonies, and one would assume that convention kept them from the polls. It is clear, however, that Negroes did vote in Virginia, North and South Carolina, but in those places, as well as in Georgia, laws eventually forbade the practice.[13]

To summarize the situation on the eve of the Revolution, we can characterize the late-colonial electorate as adult, male, Protestant, and white. Property restrictions cut down the potential electorate somewhat, but for the most part, the property requirement had become nominal and was often ignored, so that it did not constitute a bar to significant numbers of would-be voters. On the other hand, distance, deference, and indifference, (born of apathy, complacency, and cynicism and various combinations thereof) kept very large numbers of voters more-or-less voluntarily away from the polls. Thus estimates that 20 to 40 percent of the adult white males actually voted during the eighteenth century ring true. Despite this expanded electorate, many immigrants, propertyless city laborers, indentured servants, non-Protestants, and migrant frontiersmen were legally disfranchised. This made up at least 20 percent of the white adult males as late as the 1770s, and may have gone as high as 50 percent in some places.[14]

As the American Revolution approached during the 1760s and 1770s, the rhetoric of liberty and equality inevitably influenced the way colonists thought about the right to participate in government through the ballot.[15] In 1765 James Otis of Massachusetts began to undermine the stake-in-society principle when he asserted that every individual (of course, he meant adult men) had a stake in society just by living in it and valuing his "life and liberty."[16] Indeed, for some decades before the Revolution, several colonies had permitted anyone who had performed militia duty or paid taxes to vote, either condition representing sufficient commitment to his community to support his right to vote. Not only were calls for an expanded suffrage heard, but with separation from England, officers formerly appointed by the Crown now became elective. Gubernatorial contests created great excitement and brought many more voters to the polls. The statement in the Pennsylvania constitution of 1776 "that all free men having a sufficient evident common interest with, and attachment to, the community, have a right to elect officers" was only a bit ahead of its time and certainly represented the wave of the future.[17] After all, the slogan of no taxation without representation had its obverse logic — any taxpayer should be permitted to vote for representatives.

The mechanics of elections were very much affected by Revolutionary ideas. Nominations became regularized and more open; polling places became more numerous and convenient; and most significantly, the secret ballot, only sporadically used in a few scattered places before the Revolution, began to gain acceptance in most states.[18] But most important of all, the idea that legislatures should be representative in a literal sense took hold everywhere in America. The conventional British idea of mixed government with separate branches for each order of society — the monarchy, aristocracy, and the commoners — fell under the force of revolutionary thinking in America. Americans asserted that legislatures should be society writ small — tiny replications of the interests and social divisions of the state. Thus also, each legislator should represent the same number of residents — or at least voters or citizens. The most important alteration affecting the electorate to come out of the Revolution, then, related not so much to the electorate as to the bodies they elected. Though the constitutionally defined principle of one person/one vote is a phenomenon of our own time, the Revolutionary ideology was the first step in that direction.

Though universal manhood suffrage was still decades in the future, the Revolutionary era saw giant strides toward it. By the time the U.S. Constitution was ratified in 1788, about 90 percent of the adult white males met eligibility requirements in New Jersey, Pennsylvania, Georgia, North and South Carolina, New Hampshire, and most towns in Massachusetts. In Virginia, historians estimate that the proportion of the population eligible to vote ranged from 70 to 90 percent; in Maryland about 70 percent; in New York perhaps 60 percent.[19] In Rhode Island and Connecticut virtually all adult white Protestant males who owned any property at all were permitted to vote, though large numbers continued to content themselves with voting in local elections only.

The establishment of the new national government in the 1790s did not bring immediate changes in the suffrage, but a broadening tendency was accelerated by the rise of political parties and the two-party system with its hotly contested elections. New states in the Southwest, as well as Vermont and Ohio, entered the Union with nearly universal white male suffrage. A series of constitutional conventions in older states beginning in 1818 in Connecticut brought adult white male — referred to contemporaneously as "universal" — suffrage to twenty-one of the twenty-four states by 1824. (Rhode Island, Virginia and Louisiana did not have it.)[20]

Of course, what was considered universal in the 1830s would not so qualify today. But the redefinition of that term did not even begin until much later. Efforts to include blacks and women got nowhere before the Civil War, and indeed it was not until Wyoming was admitted to the Union in 1890 with female suffrage that the women's suffrage movement had any success at all.[21] It took an amendment to the U.S. Constitution in 1870 to gain the right to vote for black men; another in 1920 to get it for black and white women; and the tendency towards universal suffrage — literally, through reductio ad absurdum — was continued in the Twenty-Sixth Amendment which extended the vote to eighteen-year-olds in 1971. But these are twentieth-century developments. By the standards of a different era, the mid-1830s, Alexis de Tocqueville could state that: "At the present day the principle of the sovereignty of the people has acquired in the United States all the practical development that the imagination can conceive."[22]

NOTES

1. This is a very rough approximation. In the election of 1789 electors were chosen by the legislature in several states, and Rhode Island, New York, and North Carolina did not participate. See Ben J. Wattenberg, ed., *The Statistical History of the United States* (New York, 1976), 1071. The earliest presidential election in which all electors were chosen by popular vote was in 1836. My calculation shows about 10 percent of the total population casting votes that year. (That is, 1,505,278 voted out of a population of 15,432,000 = .097.) One estimate has 57.8 percent of those eligible casting votes in 1836, with a range of 69.2 percent in Delaware and New Jersey down to 19.2 percent in Louisiana. Ibid., 8, 1074, 1072.

2. I have surveyed works that deal with the colonies generally, but have not always searched colony or local studies. The principal works are, in chronological order: Cortland F. Bishop, *History of Elections in the American Colonies* (New York, 1893); Albert Edward McKinley, *The Suffrage Franchise in the Thirteen English Colonies in America* (Philadelphia, 1969 (1905)); Chilton Williamson, *American Suffrage: From Property to Democracy, 1760-1860* (Princeton, 1960); Jackson Turner Main, *The Social Structure of Revolutionary America* (Princeton, 1965); Robert J. Dinkin, *Voting in Provincial America: A Study of Elections in the Thirteen Colonies, 1689-1776* (Westport, Ct., 1977), and *Voting in Revolutionary America: A Study of Elections in the Original Thirteen States, 1776-1789* (Westport, Ct., 1982).

3. Dinkin, *Provincial America,* 146; Edmund S. Morgan, *Inventing the People: The Rise of Popular Sovereignty in England and America* (New York, 1988), 303.

4. A brief survey of suffrage qualifications is in Frances Fox Piven and Richard A. Cloward, *Why Americans Don't Vote* (New York, 1988), chap. 3.

5. *New York Times.* November 13, 1988, Section 1, 32. George Bush won with the votes of 27 percent of the eligible voters. The 1988 vote continues a downward trend; in 1960, 62.8 percent of eligibles voted. Unofficial returns show a total of about 90 million votes cast in a population of over 240 million, or 37 percent. It was the lowest turnout since 1924.

6. Dinkin, *Provincial America,* 146 and chap. 7 generally.

7. Benjamin Gale, quoted in Morgan, *Inventing the People,* 251n.

8. A great deal of attention has been paid to the concept and practice of deference. See John B. Kirby, "Early American Politics. The Search for Ideology: An Historiographical Analysis and Critique of the Concept of Deference," *Journal of Politics* 32 (November 1970) 4:808-38.

9. Morgan, *Inventing the People.* See the index entry "women." Legally propertied women could vote in New York and New Jersey before the American Revolution, but lost that right in the years following 1776.

10. See the discussion of stake in society and free will in Donald S. Lutz, *Popular Consent and Popular Control: Whig Political Theory in the Early State Constitutions* (Baton Rouge, 1980), 99.

11. See Morgan's discussion of economic independence in *Inventing the People,* 156.

12. These studies are summarized in Dinkin, *Provincial America,* chap. 7.

13. Ibid., 31-34.

14. Ibid., 27.

15. J.R. Pole, *Political Representation in England and the Origins of the American Republic* (Berkeley, 1966). See especially chap.3.

16. Dinkin, *Provincial America,* 209.

17. Quoted in Gordon S. Wood, *The Creation of the American Republic, 1776-1787* (Chapel Hill, 1969), 169.

18. Ibid., 120.

19. Dinkin, *Revolutionary America,* 36.

20. Richard P. McCormick, *The Second American Party System: Party Formation in the Jacksonian Era* (Chapel Hill, 1966), 29. See also Edward Pessen, *Jacksonian America: Society, Personality, and Politics* (Homewood, Ill., 1969), 155.

21. Women's suffrage did not help. Wyoming had the lowest voter turnout in presidential elections in the 1890s and early-twentieth century outside of the Deep South. Wyoming first permitted women to vote in 1869 when it became a territory.

22. Tocqueville, *Democracy In America,* ed. Phillips Bradley. (New York, 1955), I:59.

SUGGESTED READINGS

Bishop, Cortlandt F. *History of Elections in the American Colonies.* New York: Columbia College, 1893.

Dinkin, Robert J. *Voting in Provincial America: A Study of Elections in the Thirteen Colonies, 1688-1776.* Westport, Ct.: Greenwood Press, 1977.

_____. *Voting in Revolutionary America: A Study of Elections in the Original Thirteen States, 1776-1789.* Westport, Ct.: Greenwood Press, 1982.

Lutz, Donald S. *Popular Consent and Popular Control: Whig Political Theory in the Early State Constitutions.* Baton Rouge: Louisiana State University Press, 1980.

Main, Jackson Turner. *The Social Structure of Revolutionary America.* Princeton: Princeton University Press, 1965.

McKinley, Albert Edward. *The Suffrage Franchise in the Thirteen English Colonies in America.* Philadelphia, Burt Franklin, 1969 (1905).

Morgan, Edmund S. *Inventing the People: The Rise of Popular Sovereignty in England and America.* New York: W.W. Norton & Company, 1988.

Pole, J.R. *Political Representation in England and the Origins of the American Republic.* Berkeley: The University of California Press, 1966.

Williamson, Chilton. *American Suffrage: From Property to Democracy, 1776-1860.* Princeton: Princeton University Press, 1960.

Campaign ribbons endorsing William Henry Harrison for president of the United States in 1840. Harrison's campaign was a landmark in American political history, as it introduced the "log cabin" image emphasizing a presidential candidate's humble origins. This image was designed to appeal to the growing ranks of "common men" who were becoming voters as the result of suffrage expansion during the early-nineteenth century. *Source: Museum of American Political Life, University of Hartford.*

2 PROPERTY AND POWER: SUFFRAGE REFORM IN THE UNITED STATES, 1787-1860

Sean Wilentz
Princeton University

During the first half of the nineteenth century, democratic forces transformed American politics. The transformation ushered in a new political era, sometimes called "the age of the common man," an era that triumphed during the presidency of Andrew Jackson (1829-1837). In this new age, Romantic ideas about the equality of men replaced the colonial attitudes of social deference. Ordinary men ceased deferring to the social elite, and they began asserting themselves in all facets of life. In particular, ordinary men plunged into electoral politics by the thousands, driving voter turnout rates in national elections to historically high levels, between roughly 70 and 80 percent beginning with the presidential election of 1840.

Important institutional and legal changes which opened up the political process to popular participation both underlay and resulted from "the age of the common man." The number of elective offices on the state level expanded. Political parties became instruments of mass political mobilization, rather than tools of the elite. And most significantly, state after state eliminated property requirements for voting, producing an electoral system based on universal white manhood suffrage. Contemporaries considered suffrage expansion as one of the most important democratic achievements of the era.

Americans of the mid-nineteenth century — and even of today — regarded the establishment of universal white manhood suffrage as an expression of the uniquely democratic spirit of American politics, a spirit that was planted by the American Revolution and blossomed during "the age of the common man." But as Sean Wilentz explains in this essay, the suffrage reforms of the 1810s, 1820s, and 1830s had origins that went beyond the American Revolutionary tradition. Early-nineteenth-century suffrage reform drew upon a transatlantic traffic in political ideas, he says. More important, the reforms received a strong boost from the commercial revolution which produced massive economic changes both in the United States and abroad. According to Wilentz, the commercial revolution brought about a cash-based market economy, a development which transformed American politics and reshaped Americans' conception of the right to vote.

Voting and American Democracy

etween 1787 and 1860, American politics underwent a decisive democratic transformation, signalled by the achievement of white manhood suffrage. Few politicians at the time could avoid coming to terms with the democratizing trend; ever since, it has received considerable attention from historians. Even so, we have yet to comprehend fully the ramifications of early suffrage reform. More than a passing development, the proliferation of democratic reforms in the early-nineteenth century ushered in the first long cycle of a seemingly endless battle over the first principles of American politics. The reformers' strivings were of international as well as national importance; their success was tied to a dramatic revolution in American economic and social relations; their movements were rooted in popular political agitation that has yet to receive its due credit. And reform had its darker ironies as well — ironies that, for a time, drained the cause of popular sovereignty of its expansive, universalizing power.

The historian Chilton Williamson's description of the shift "from property to democracy" captures the essentials of late-eighteenth and early-nineteenth century suffrage reform.[1] At the end of the American Revolution, most of the states required some sort of property ownership as a prerequisite for voting, often in the form of a freehold title in land. Politics operated through networks of elite power and deferential popular participation; according to received opinion, no man without property deserved the franchise. By 1860, in contrast, virtually every state had adopted universal white manhood suffrage, or its rough equivalent.

There is a danger in misrepresenting what these reforms actually accomplished. Given the relatively wide diffusion of landed property among free American households in the eighteenth century, suffrage requirements that might seem stiff in retrospect were actually far less so. Estimates suggest that, on the eve of the Revolution, somewhere between 50 and 75 percent of all adult free males could vote, at least for some offices. Many of those excluded were young men, who fully expected to inherit or otherwise accumulate sufficient property to make them full political citizens. Nevertheless, to divorce formal political rights from property ownership — breaking with the venerable "stake-in-society" principle — was a philosophical transition of no small moment. It would loom even larger in the nineteenth century, as early industrialization and immigration augmented the numbers of poor and propertyless free American men.

The democratic impulses unleashed by the popular mobilizations of the Revolution initiated the first steps toward widening the suffrage. Between 1776 and 1783, significant reforms took place in Pennsylvania, New Hampshire, New Jersey, Georgia, and Maryland, while demands for reforms — including universal suffrage — surfaced else-where. But to say (as some historians have) that the Revolution com-mitted the country to democracy is an exaggeration. In one key state, Massachusetts, the Revolution actually brought a reactionary turn vis-a-vis voting rights by stiffening property qualifications. New York's constitution of 1777 instituted a double-tiered system of property requirements for elections to the upper and lower legislative houses. Other states, like Virginia, retained their colonial property require-ments. After the war, Vermont's admission to the union brought in the first state without any formal property tests, while in Delaware, Georgia, and North Carolina, taxpaying requirements replaced older property laws — a de facto form of white manhood suffrage. Still, between 1783 and 1800, no previously existing state completely sev-ered property from voting.

Thereafter, democratic reforms proceeded in four successive waves. The first wave, from 1801 to the War of 1812, brought reductions in property requirements in Maryland, South Carolina, and New Jersey, but the defeat of similar efforts in Massachusetts, Rhode Island, Con-necticut, and New York. In the western territories, as late as 1812, only one new state, Kentucky, had been admitted to the Union with-out some sort of property stipulation. The second wave, lasting from 1815 to 1828, was far more powerful, especially in the Northeast, where reformers won major victories in Connecticut, Massachusetts, and New York. By 1828, the year of Andrew Jackson's election, property barriers remained formidable only in Rhode Island, Louisiana, Virginia, and (in upper house elections) North Carolina.

A third, largely southern reform wave began with the momentous Virginia constitutional convention of 1829-30, which finally revised that state's freehold requirements. Thereafter, a string of reform con-ventions in Mississippi, North Carolina, and Georgia further democ-ratized voting. Finally, Rhode Island's famous Dorr War in the 1840s sparked a fourth series of efforts, in which several states that had not yet done so ended all forms of property tests for adult white males.

These reforms did not eliminate all restrictive procedures, even within the white male electorate. Residency requirements, registry laws, poll taxes, alien voting, and naturalization procedures (among other things) would remain sticky problems long after the Civil War. Nevertheless, as Williamson remarked: "it was an impressive fact, of world significance, that the movement to eliminate property as a test for voting had achieved so great a degree of success by 1860."[2] How, though, are we to judge that significance?

We should not, by any means, assume that these events were unique-ly American, or that they transpired in pristine isolation from democratic movements abroad. Americans were not the only people to institute manhood suffrage before 1860: the French did as well, after their revolution in 1848. And Americans were neither uninformed nor uninterested in democratic advances elsewhere. Although beholden to the ideals of the Revolution, American suffrage reform came about not as the outcome of an insular battle, but as part of a confluence of global events.

From the start, all sides in the American suffrage debates drew on ideas received from the Old World — or, more exactly, on ideas that crisscrossed the Atlantic as part of an international conversation. Down to the 1820s, opponents to reform took as their first line of defense the arguments derived from the eighteenth-century British Tory William Blackstone, that the suffrage ought to exclude those men of mean circumstances whom Blackstone assumed had no political will of their own.

As late as the 1830s and 1840s, Blackstonian ideas found their champions as far west as the wilds of Illinois and Louisiana. Younger conservatives turned away from Blackstone in the early decades of the nineteenth century, only to seize upon the writings of another English writer, the seventeenth-century republican James Harrington.

Suffrage reformers, for their part, sometimes seemed to want to break entirely from all Old World precedents. Yet that very argument, along with some of the specifics of reform agendas, borrowed liberally from the ideas of various seventeenth- and eighteenth-century British writers. Among these were the almost universally cited thoughts of Algernon Sydney and John Locke — but also the legacy of another more radical tradition stretching back to the English Revolution, the New Model Army, and Levellers, and the famous Putney debates, and filtered through the writings of such later radicals as the Englishman Major John Cartwright and the eighteenth-century international revolutionary Thomas Paine.

American reformers also took heart — and instruction — from their own contemporaries abroad. In at least one case — Abraham Bishop of Connecticut — direct contact with democratic ideas during a grand tour of France in the 1780s proved the personal turning point in the making of a reformer. Other Americans were well aware of transatlantic movements, and they drew a parallel between the two situations. In 1808-09, South Carolina newspapers cited the works of the British reformer John Horne Tooke and the activities of the Society of United Irishmen, along with quotations from Paine. Prior to New York's constitutional convention of 1812, Albany and New York City newspapers carried writings and speeches by William Cobbett, "Orator" Henry Hunt, and other British activists on the need for reform; so, a decade later, did Virginia newspapers on the eve of that state's revision of the suffrage. In Mississippi, the impetus for suffrage reform in 1831 came directly from the French Revolution of the previous year and the continuing British movement for parliamentary reform.

This traffic in ideas was hardly one-way: reformers overseas (especially in Britain) were greatly emboldened by the writings and achievements of the Americans. Nor were the American debates conducted at the rarified level of a seminar on political theory. Nevertheless, when they did talk about ideas, Americans spoke in an informal, international lexicon of democratic politics that blossomed throughout the Atlantic world — and not just the United States — in the first half of the nineteenth century.

Of course, outside of Rhode Island, reform came to the American states far more peaceably and swiftly than elsewhere. For a variety of reasons, social and political, the kind of landed conservative opposition to democratization that proved so powerful in other countries never consolidated itself here. This is not to say, however, that democratic reform was an inevitable outcome of existing American social conditions. Vast social changes were necessary before the deferential politics of the eighteenth century gave way to the democratic politics of the 1820s and after.

Recent historians have described these changes in terms of a market revolution. Between, roughly, 1800 and 1850, an astonishing series of economic innovations hastened the spread of wage labor and commercial agriculture in the northern states and the spread of plantation slavery in the South. New financial institutions, transportation improvements, and the rapid accumulation of American merchant capital shattered old artisanal and yeoman social relations, and tied more and more Americans to an impersonal cash market. With these changes, old social resentments mingled with new ones, to propel entire classes of people — urban workingmen, manufacturers, yeomen, planters, financiers, petty slave holders — into political battles over issues like debtor relief, banking, internal improvements, tariffs, temperance, and (ultimately) slavery.

Connections between the market revolution and democratization can be discovered at several levels. The emergence of new local elites who came from outside the established gentry — urban and country merchants, manufacturers, lawyers, newspaper editors, and other professionals — clearly increased the pressure for change. Throughout the country, in various walks of life, there arose an articulate stratum of ambitious men who owed little or nothing to the old ideal of a landed freeholder citizenry and a benign, virtuous patrician leadership. In state after state, these new men of the market revolution played critical roles, either in mobilizing support for reforms or in helping broker these reforms in state legislatures and constitutional conventions.

At another level, the suffrage debates tapped into the broader social resentments that accompanied the market revolution. As the historian Daniel Rodgers has noted, the language of expanded popular sovereignty sprang with particular passion from the mouths of those whom President Andrew Jackson called the "real people": "men of little property shut out of the early political arrangements of power, farmers and petty planters from the malapportioned back countries, debtors far from the seats of legal justice, urban mechanics grown restless with the politics of deference and the injuries of merchant capitalism." Inexorably, the issues of democratic rights became entwined with the popular perception that some Americans, by dint of their economic privileges, were at war with popular sovereignty itself. As a brake on the power of the unproductive few, spokesmen for the so-called "real people" demanded an expansion of democracy.

In the 1830s, the Democratic Party became the chief carrier and promoter of these perceptions. But outside of party politics, as well as inside, the social conflicts caused by the market revolution kept intruding on public affairs. In the South, clashes between "up-country" yeomen and "low-country" planters and their urban allies fed directly into the politics of suffrage, most conspicuously in Virginia. In the newer western states, reforming politicians mixed opportunism and idealism to build strong bases of support in less commercialized regions. In the Northeast, testy coalitions of urban workingmen, small farmers in remote districts, and new manufacturing/commercial interests bent on reform, became the backbone of the reform constituencies.

Only in Rhode Island did these social and political fault lines crack open in a violent convulsion. During the early 1840s, Rhode Island split into rival factions regarding reform of the state constitution, with the broadening of suffrage as one of the central questions. The main suffrage-expansion advocate, Thomas W. Dorr, led followers on a military assault of the state capitol building in Providence, after he failed to establish himself as governor following an election in 1842. Dorr was defeated and fled the state, and conservatives begrudged only small concessions on suffrage.

Elsewhere, state legislatures or constitutional conventions settled differences peacefully. These proceedings, especially the conventions in large states like New York and Virginia, have received a good deal of attention, as symbols of judicious, pragmatic American politics. In many instances, however, these assemblies would have been unimaginable without persistent political pressure from below.

Popular expressions for democratic reform assumed a variety of forms. Town and legislative petitioning over matters like the placement of polling places — a more or less constant occurrence in post-Revolutionary America — may seem to have been unimportant. Yet they also showed something of how local electors were vigilant about securing their vote, in an era where simply getting to the polls over rough country roads was not always easy. Of more obvious importance were the town and county petitions which flooded into state legislatures, the state constitutional conventions, and (from the western territories) the U.S. Congress, with various demands for changes in the voting laws. Enfranchised voters sympathetic to reform had the additional weapon of their ballots.

Most interesting of all were those efforts which inaugurated state and local reforms. Sometimes, these began as spontaneous efforts by like-minded neighbors — as, in 1801, when a group of cartmen in New York City, angered that the Federalist-dominated municipal government would not grant them the freemanship required to vote in city elections, complained to the mayor and aldermen. (A few years later they won their case, under a Jeffersonian administration.) Far more impressive mobilizations preceded the state-by-state reforms of the 1820s and 1830s. In New York, popular reform assemblies met in Washington County in 1817, and in Montgomery County three years later. On July 4, 1820, numerous mass meetings were held around the state to call for the extension of the vote to all taxpayers and all members of the militia. Even more dramatic events unfolded in Virginia. In 1815, nearly fifteen years before the calling of the Virginia state constitutional convention, a group of nonfreeholders met in Harrisonburg, and prepared a circular reform petition for distribution around the state. A year later, a mass meeting at Winchester described the state's constitution as an "absolute mockery of free government." Popular agitation, though frustrated for several years more, did not die. On the eve of the state convention in 1829, talk at a mass meeting of nonfreeholders prompted newspaper discussions of the desirability of forming a physical force party, to secure the changes that thus far had been thwarted.

On other occasions popular unrest threatened even more ominously to step beyond the boundaries of the law. The Rhode Island example — which degenerated into a civil insurrection — was the most spectacular, but it was hardly the only case in which the unenfranchised organized to take matters into their own hands. In 1822 and 1823, the newspapers of North Carolina backcountry were filled with appeals for a popularly-constituted illicit state convention to gain electoral reform. Ten years later, a local convention met in Hancock County, Georgia, and called for the people of that state to hold their own constitutional convention. To head off a political rupture, the Georgia legislature eventually scheduled a legal convention, which met in 1833. Under pressure for further reform and threats of illegal assemblies, the legislature called yet another convention in 1839. To be sure, not every state was gripped with popular reform enthusiasm. In those that were, though, democratization came about not as a free gift from political elites, but in part from organized efforts outside the halls of power.

In sum, the success of democratic reform reflected both the legacy of the Revolution and the disruptive effects of social change and popular engagement. Nonetheless, it also reflected the limits of popular sovereignty, as understood even by reformers. In several ways, the formal democratization of politics, while hardly a sham, proved dangerously and in some ways oppressively incomplete by the Civil War era.

Soon after various reforms fell into place, some Americans questioned whether the widening of the suffrage actually affected the structure of power. Workingmen radicals of the 1830s and 1840s raised the matter most insistently, claiming that merely abolishing property restrictions would not in itself rid the country of those monied men whom they called the "mushroom aristocracy." In some places, the success of suffrage reform brought only a subsequent decline in voting and interest in further political reforms. It seemed, as one newspaper reported, that the political elites had "disarmed the poorer classes by taking them into the body politic."[3]

For many other Americans, meanwhile, the expansion of white male suffrage could look like the very antithesis of democracy. Women, for example, had been given no thought as citizens before the American Revolution: thereafter, on those rare occasions when male suffrage reformers even broached the subject of women's suffrage, it was usually dismissed with misogynist contempt. Only in the 1840s did supporters of woman suffrage begin to find a collective voice — and of course, even then, they faced a long and rocky road before they would be heeded. Black men, meanwhile, had even more reason to resent the immediate fruits of antebellum democratization. In state after state where, after the Revolution, free black men enjoyed some sort of franchise, but the years from 1800 to 1850 saw the steady erosion of such rights, to the point of extinction. Southern reform spokesmen made no bones about their claims that democratization was a means to ensure greater unity among whites (and hence greater security for the institution of slavery) to be gained at the expense of that section's free black population. In the North, a blend of political expediency and heightened popular racism promoted a crackdown on the black franchise. On the eve of the Civil War, the overwhelming majority of northern states denied blacks the vote.

By the 1850s, meanwhile, the politics of democratization had lost much of the popular zeal of earlier decades. After the war with Mexico in 1846, the issue of popular sovereignty became entangled, as never before, with questions surrounding territorial rights and the expansion of slavery. The moral and ideological passions surrounding the slavery issue threatened to cut across the political allegiances formed in response to the market revolution; consequently, the rhetoric of democracy became ever more closely linked with centrist efforts to keep the slavery issue out of national affairs and to paper over the sectional division with compromises and soothing words. If any national figure stood as the great champion of popular sovereignty in the mid-1850s, it was Illinois politician Stephen A. Douglas, who turned the phrase to mean accepting slavery where it existed, and where it did not, putting its existence to the vote of the people. As hard as he tried, Douglas could not make this formula work. Only after the Civil War that followed would the suffrage and related issues of popular sovereignty reemerge as the flashpoints of American politics.

The story, of course, does not end there. Through the first post-Civil War Reconstruction of the 1860s and 1870s, the era of black disfranchisement in the 1890s and on to the second Reconstruction of the Civil Rights Movement in the 1950s and 1960s, the issue of suffrage rights remained central to the struggles of black Americans. So, as other groups of Americans pressed their claims for power, they turned first and foremost to securing, and sometimes recovering, their right to vote. That they eventually succeeded is surely a mark of American democracy's maturation. That it took them so long is a sobering lesson about the American past. And how much suffrage reform has changed the structure and exercise of power in the United States remains an abiding question for the present and the future.

NOTES

1. Chilton Williamson, *American Suffrage from Property to Democracy 1760-1860* (Princeton, NJ, 1960).

2. Ibid., 280.

3. *National Advocate* [New York], August 18, 1821.

SUGGESTED READINGS

Chute, Marchette Gaylord. *The First Liberty: A History of the Right to Vote in America, 1619-1850.* New York: Dutton, 1969.

Morgan, Edmund S. *Inventing the People: The Rise of Popular Sovereignty in England and America.* New York: W. W. Norton & Company, 1988.

Peterson, Merrill D., ed., *Democracy, Liberty, and Property: The State Constitutional Conventions of the 1820s.* Indianapolis: Bobbs-Merrill, 1966.

Williamson, Chilton. *American Suffrage From Property to Democracy, 1760-1860.* Princeton: Princeton University Press, 1960.

Political ribbons, circa 1844, supporting the Native American party of Philadelphia. Opposed to the growing political influence of Irish Catholic immigrants, the Native American party and later the Know Nothing party called for federal legislation to lengthen the period of residence required before each Irish immigrant could become a naturalized citizen. Lengthening residence requirements for citizenship status would have delayed immigrants' eligibility to vote. *Source: Museum of American Political Life, University of Hartford.*

3 Defining Citizenship: Immigration and the Struggle for Voting Rights in Antebellum America

Paul Kleppner
Northern Illinois University

The United States is a nation of immigrants, and this was especially true for the century running from 1820 to 1920 when more than twenty-one million newcomers arrived on America's shores. The rate of immigration was particularly high during two periods of this century: the four decades preceding the start of the American Civil War in 1861 and the three decades preceding U.S. military entry into World War I in 1917. During the first of these two periods, the years 1820 to 1861, about two million Irish and a million German immigrants settled in the United States, igniting a fierce social controversy: how would these new people be incorporated into the mainstream of American life?

As Paul Kleppner explains in the essay that follows, native-born Americans' reaction to massive Irish and German immigration ran counter to the early-nineteenth-century drive for universal white manhood suffrage. Because these immigrants were so different from the American mainstream in terms of religion (they were predominantly Roman Catholic rather than Protestant), socioeconomic standing (they were mainly peasants and unskilled laborers, rather than solid yeoman farmers or urban artisans), and national culture (they were still proudly Irish or German, rather than loyally "American"), some Americans questioned whether immigrants should be granted the full rights of citizenship without a long apprenticeship to learn about American values, history and institutions. In the 1840s and 1850s, these concerns led to a major political struggle, in which "nativist" politicians sought to extend the naturalization period, thereby curtailing immigrants' right to vote and to participate in the political community. But as Professor Kleppner maintains, this struggle ultimately ended in failure, establishing once and for all that immigrants to the United States should be assured of full citizenship rights, especially the right to vote.

I n July 1988, the Democratic National Convention celebrated the American dream. Entering the convention hall as his Jewish father-in-law conducted the orchestra's rendition of the popular song, "Coming to America," Massachusetts Governor Michael S. Dukakis, the son of Greek immigrant parents, presented himself as the proud personification of that dream. "A dream," he said, "that brought my father to this country seventy-six years ago; that brought Mother and her family here one year later — poor, unable to speak English; but with a burning desire to succeed in their new land of opportunity." And succeed they did, for their son was addressing his party's convention as its nominee for the presidency of the United States.

The parents of Governor Dukakis came to this country early in the twentieth century, as part of the third and largest wave of European immigration. They were two of the more than twenty-one million newcomers who reached these shores between 1820 and 1924, when Congress permanently limited the number of immigrants to be admitted annually. This rapid influx of immigrants, mainly Catholics and Jews from southern and eastern Europe, and their highly visible concentration in the nation's cities, sparked an outburst of anti-foreign sentiment called "nativism" around the turn of the century.

Those who feared and fought against this new immigration scored a number of short-term victories in the 1910s and 1920s. They imposed the Prohibition Amendment on the nation, outlawing the manufacture, sale, and distribution of alcoholic beverages, and they limited future immigration by establishing a quota system based on the 1890 census which had been completed before most of the new immigrants had arrived. They also undertook a massive campaign to "Americanize" these newcomers, an effort that involved revising the curriculum and instructional materials used in the public schools along with an extensive program of adult education. In all of this, they assumed the superiority of their version of American culture. The customs and traditions that these new immigrants brought with them were to be altered, to be brought into conformity with what the Americanizers thought were proper values and behavior. If Michael Dukakis's father Panos and other members of his generation of immigrants felt that they were viewed as inferiors and consigned to second-class status, then they had good reasons for believing so.

While nativist sentiment around the turn of the century was powerful, and while it aimed at limiting the activities of immigrants in a number of ways, it did not make any serious effort to undermine immigrants' political rights. True, many states adopted literacy tests and personal registration requirements that were aimed at these newcomers. But creating new procedural barriers to the exercise of the franchise was quite different from flatly denying these people the right to vote. Their right to become citizens, and their right as citizens to vote, was secure because those battles had been fought and won by an earlier generation of immigrants that had faced an even more virulent wave of nativist sentiment during the 1840s and 1850s.

In colonial and postrevolutionary America, the concepts of citizenship and voting were not linked. Voting eligibility then depended primarily upon property owning. But as the states first reduced and later eliminated this economic barrier, they made other substantive qualifications, including citizenship, explicit. New Hampshire enacted the first citizenship requirement in 1814, and its example was followed by Connecticut and Virginia in 1818, by New Jersey in 1820, by Massachusetts and New York two years later, and by Delaware, North Carolina, and Rhode Island within the following two decades. With the exception of Vermont, Tennessee, and Ohio, which did not adopt citizenship requirements until 1828, 1834 and 1852, respectively, all of the new states entered the Union with a citizenship requirement in their constitutions or election codes. Only Georgia and South Carolina failed to link voting with citizenship prior to 1860.

With voting rights securely linked to citizenship, the question of voter eligibility for immigrants pivoted on the details of the naturalization process. The first federal naturalization act of 1790 was a reasonably liberal one, requiring only a two-year period of residence in the country before qualifying for citizenship. The Naturalization Act of 1795 increased the period of residence to five years, but even this longer period failed to satisfy those who feared that immigration threatened the country's homogeneity and their own political control. Taking advantage of their majority in Congress, the Federalists in 1798 amended the Naturalization Act to increase the period of residence to fourteen years.

With the triumph of Jefferson and his supporters in the election of 1800, however, this restrictive measure was quickly repealed. The new law of 1802, which was the last major piece of legislation on the subject during the nineteenth century, reinstated the general requirements of the act of 1795, including the residence period of five years.

While Federalists and Jeffersonians disagreed over the details of naturalization policy, they shared the central belief that lay at its core. They both believed that some term of residence, or period of apprenticeship, was required before conferring the privileges and immunities of citizenship upon immigrants. This was, both sides agreed, the surest way of guaranteeing an alien's attachment to the country and adoption of the habits and values of its new republican life.

Because voting became linked to citizenship, and citizenship was linked to naturalization, the efforts in the 1840s and 1850s to limit the voting rights of immigrants mainly targeted the naturalization process. These efforts aimed especially at lengthening the period of residence, usually to twenty-one years, the time required for a native-born citizen to reach voting age. And these efforts were only part of a larger movement aimed at preserving native-stock culture and customs in the face of a floodtide of immigration from Europe, especially from Germany and Ireland.

During the 1830s, only 552,000 immigrants reached the United States. In the following decade, the number of new arrivals tripled to 1.5 million; and it nearly doubled again during the 1850s, reaching 2.7 million. Under any circumstances, numbers of this order would have strained the absorptive capacity of a fledgling nation whose total population was only 12 million in 1830.

Straining that capacity even further, however, was the fact that the character of the immigration also changed, compared to the character of new arrivals during colonial years and the early 1800s. By the 1850s, persons with urban backgrounds and occupations, mechanics and laborers mostly, greatly outnumbered farmers. And newcomers from the Protestant parts of Great Britain and northern Ireland came to be outnumbered by immigrants from Catholic Ireland and the German states. This shift had begun during the 1830s; its pace quickened during the 1840s; and during the next decade southern Ireland and the German states accounted for six out of every ten of the country's newcomers.

These newly arriving immigrants did not blend easily into the country's social fabric. There were simply too many of them, coming too quickly, for that to occur. Besides, when they settled down, they tended to concentrate mostly in the eastern and midwestern states. And within these states, they lived together creating enclaves of settlement, mainly in cities.

Living apart from others, adhering to different values, and practicing different mores and customs, these newcomers quickly caught the attention of native-stock Americans. The alarm went out even in the 1830s, before immigration reached its high point and while it was still mainly from Great Britain and Protestant Ireland. In the late summer and autumn of 1834, Samuel F. B. Morse, who would become better known as the inventor of the telegraph, published a series of letters in the New York *Observer,* warning that the Catholic monarchies of Europe were sending immigrants to take over this country and force it to succumb to the doctrines of despotism and popery. In his powerful sermon published in 1835 as *A Plea for the*

West, the Reverend Lyman Beecher echoed Morse's fears of a papal plot to conquer the United States through immigration.

However farfetched and even paranoid we might judge these views of a plot to overthrow the country's democratic institutions, they enjoyed great popularity at the time. The arguments by Morse and Beecher tapped popular beliefs, gave new urgency to them, and thus aroused and mobilized popular opinion. Moreover, while both talked in particular about a papal conspiracy, their arguments linked immigration and Catholicism and made both equally objectionable to many natives.

Much of the nativist literature of the 1830s concentrated on this conspiracy theme. And a good deal of it, like Rebecca Reed's *Six Months in a Convent* (1835), or Maria Monk's *Awful Disclosures of the Hotel Dieu Nunnery of Montreal* (1836), featured lurid, even pornographic accounts of intimate relationships between priests and nuns.

The literature of the next decades was mild by comparison, although it never wholly lost its conspiratorial motif or abandoned sensational sexual exposes. But there was a clear shift in the overall tone and presumed targets of the appeals. More attention was given to substantive matters, such as disputes between Protestants and Catholics over Bible reading in public schools, and over the use of public funds to support private church-affiliated schools. Even more important, however, the literature of the early 1840s began to express a generalized fear of immigration, a sense that these newcomers, Protestant as well as Catholic, threatened America's institutions and its way of life.

The general argument against immigration had several subthemes, not all of which were consistent with the others. First, nativists pointed to the impoverished condition of the newcomers. Most immigrants were poor, their meager resources exhausted by the cost of passage, and at best they were employable only as common laborers, earning wages barely enough to keep them going. The great danger, then, was that they would become paupers, to be supported by hardworking, taxpaying citizens. Second, nativists often argued that the foreign-born competed with American workers for good jobs and that their presence in large numbers kept wages low for all workers. Third, immigrants were undermining the country's moral standards through their disrespect for the Puritan Sabbath and their drinking habits. Finally, nativists blamed the lawlessness and disorder that they saw throughout society on what they regarded as the morally dissolute condition of the immigrants.

In shifting away from the titillating sexual exposes of the 1830s, nativists intended to broaden their audience. By the middle of the

1840s, they were using arguments designed to appeal to the country's respectable, church-going middle and upper-middle classes. The specters of increased pauperism, job and wage competition, decaying morality, and rampant lawlessness were aimed at these audiences.

The country's organized religious groups needed little prodding. They had long complained of what they regarded as ungodly and immoral behavior on the part of immigrants, whom they generally stigmatized as "infidels" or "Papists." Moreover, they routinely warned that such newcomers "are inimical to our civil and political institutions." It was this final linkage, that immigration posed a danger to the country's civil and political institutions, that led nativists to political action. Immigration, as they saw it, produced massive political corruption, with immigrants voting as a bloc, often under the direction of their Catholic or Lutheran priests. Moreover, since they thought that both major parties pandered to the "foreign vote," nativists created their own political organizations to eliminate this threat to republican principles.

Political parties dedicated to nativist principles appeared in a number of locales in the late 1830s and early 1840s. Typically, these were local organizations that arose in response to the growing size and political involvement of the immigrant population in their communities. While nativist parties enjoyed success in places like Lexington, St. Louis, Philadelphia, and New York City, efforts by local leaders to create a permanent national organization failed, and the Native American party, as it ultimately named itself, passed out of existence in 1848.

While the nativists of the 1840s were a diverse lot, they agreed on basic principles. They opposed the existing naturalization laws, arguing that five years was too short a time for immigrants to learn the habits and values of republican life. They proposed increasing the waiting period to twenty-one years, the length of time native-born inhabitants had to live in the country before qualifying to vote. Second, they agreed that only native-born Americans should be eligible to hold public offices. Thus, after waiting twenty-one years, immigrants would be naturalized at best into a second-class citizenship, eligible to vote but never eligible to be elected or appointed to public office.

When the Native American party expired in the late 1840s, nativists concentrated their energies on building a network of social organizations. They formed a series of secret societies complete with rituals, symbols, handclasps and passwords known only to initiates. Until the early 1850s, these organizations worked covertly to influence the processes of selecting candidates within both major parties. By 1854 this network served as the organizational base for another anti-immigrant political party, the Know Nothing party.

The precise origins of the Know Nothings are not clear. The party's roots run directly to the Order of the Star Spangled Banner, a secret society founded in New York City in 1849. In turn, this organization may have had its origins in the Order of United Americans, a secret benevolent and patriotic society that had been created in New York City in 1844. In any case, the order's popular name was pinned on it by the New York *Tribune* because its members responded to questions about its rituals and mysteries by saying, "I know nothing."

The Know Nothing order initially functioned as an interest group, secretly endorsing candidates supporting nativist principles. By 1853 in some locales, and the following year in even more, the order crossed the line from pressure group to political party, operating now in the open to nominate and campaign for its own candidates. In the process, its success astounded its enemies, and sometimes its own leaders as well, and shook the country's political system to its roots.

Between 1853 and 1856, the Know Nothings enjoyed spectacular success. The party captured the governorship and almost every seat in the Massachusetts legislature in 1854, won a surprising statewide victory in Pennsylvania, and made an impressive showing in New York State and in local elections in Connecticut. In the following year, Know Nothings won control of all the New England states except Maine and Vermont and emerged as the leading opposition to the Democrats in the Middle Atlantic states, California, and such slave states as Alabama, Georgia, Kentucky, Louisiana, Maryland, Mississippi, Tennessee, and Virginia. And in 1856, just three years after the party began open activity, its candidate for the presidency, Millard Fillmore, polled nearly 900,000 votes, over 21 percent of the total, which was a larger share of the vote than any other third-party candidate in our history except Theodore Roosevelt in 1912.

The meteoric rise of the Know Nothings contributed to a major reorientation of national politics during the 1850s. In particular, it sounded the death knell for the Whig party, which had emerged during the 1830s in opposition to the leading political party of the time, the Democrats led by President Andrew Jackson. Beset by desertions on all fronts, by free soilers, temperance supporters, and nativists, Whiggery collapsed. By 1856 the nation's electoral system was in disarray, with one of its major parties, the Whigs, disappearing and its successor, the modern Republican party, still struggling to be born.

It is beyond our immediate purpose to examine the complex political events of the 1850s, events which ultimately culminated in secession and civil war. But to understand the Know Nothing political party, and to assess its impact on immigrant voting rights, we need to pose questions that go beyond descriptive details. Who were the

Know Nothings, from what economic and social origins did they come, and what political aims did they seek? Why did they enjoy such sudden success, only to disappear almost as suddenly? And what was the legacy of the Know Nothings, what did they accomplish?

The Know Nothing, or American party as it called itself by 1856, was first and foremost an anti-Catholic party. The organization's literature and self-descriptions leave no doubt about that.

But when Know Nothings suggested remedies, their proposals threatened all immigrants. As the Native Americans had in the 1840s, the Know Nothings advocated a twenty-one year probationary period prior to naturalization. They also advocated limiting public office holding to native-born citizens. Finally, they believed that only native-born Americans should have the right to vote.

It is not surprising that there was considerable continuity of purpose and policy aims between the nativist movements of the 1840s and 1850s. The impulses and parties of both decades seem to have drawn their leaders and supporters from the same economic and social sources.

What we know about the members of Know Nothing lodges indicates that the movement enlisted mainly middling and quite average men. The Massachusetts lodges, for example, enlisted mainly manual workers and artisans, and the leaders of Pittsburgh's Know Nothing party were mainly artisans and clerks. Often scorned by their opponents as rabble and thugs, Know Nothingism actually seems to have been a movement of solid, respectable, native Protestant, working- and middle-class citizens.

The populist quality of Know Nothingism was also clear in the movement's rejection of party politicians and established party organizations. Know Nothing leaders and office-holders were mainly young, inexperienced men, not the seasoned politicians who had dominated these levels of activity in the Democratic and Whig parties. Know Nothings were also contemptuous of existing party organizations, perceiving them as unable or unwilling to tackle what they regarded as the critical issue of the day.

Dissatisfaction with politics as usual and a desire for new leadership were widespread sentiments in the 1850s. And the Know Nothings' appeal to these sentiments was a critical factor underlying their sudden success.

Despite their meteoric rise, the Know Nothings were not able to achieve their major policy aims. While bills were introduced in both the U.S. Senate and House to increase the waiting period to twenty-one years prior to naturalization, Know Nothings lacked the support even to bring these measures to a vote.

They scored somewhat more success at the state level. In both Connecticut and Massachusetts, for example, Know Nothing legislatures disbanded local militia companies composed of immigrant members. In both of these states, they also secured constitutional amendments prescribing that the ability to read the constitution or statutes of the state should be a requirement for exercising the right to vote. Otherwise, however, for all of their fury and ferocity, Know Nothings were not able to alter the country's basic policies on immigration and naturalization.

Numerous factors contributed to the demise of the Know Nothings. Their early success attracted old-fashioned politicians who grabbed the party's label but were indifferent, or even hostile, to its principles. The appearance of these old-line politicos, in turn, disillusioned those who saw Know Nothingism as a means of repudiating the old parties and returning power to the people. At the same time, continuing disagreements over secrecy weakened the party internally. Its association in some cities with violent gangs of street thugs who assaulted naturalized citizens on their way to the polls, and the weak performance of Know Nothing legislatures and city councils, served to discredit the party. Even more significantly, large numbers of its grassroots supporters were recruited into the ranks of a less narrow and more inclusive popular front movement aimed at defeating the Democrats, a movement which eventually coalesced into the Republican party.

Finally, the drive for victory at the polls also helped to end the Know Nothing clamor. Needing votes from foreign-born citizens in many locales, pragmatic politicians simply could not allow themselves and their organizations to be identified exclusively with nativism. Whig leaders had begun to do their electoral arithmetic by the early 1850s, and they appealed to immigrant voters. Dismayed by these attempts by Whigs to build an inclusive coalition, nativists abandoned their old partisan ally and built their own political organization. Pragmatic Republican party builders were even more sensitive to the need to build an inclusive coalition. Thus, while welcoming those who earlier had supported the Know Nothings, they labored mightily, and successfully in most places, to avoid being tarred with the image of nativism. To be sure, they were not always completely victorious, and there would be a continuing tension within the Republican party throughout the rest of the century between the pragmatists, who sought always to broaden the party's appeal to the country's diverse social groups, and those who thought it should stand foursquare for the principles that the Know Nothings, and the Native Americans before them, had espoused.

In the end, of course, the pragmatists won, and for the same reason that the Know Nothings in the 1850s failed to achieve their aims. Armed with citizenship and the right to vote, naturalized immigrants trooped to the polls and defended themselves. They quickly and unerringly identified their political friends and enemies, and used the most effective weapon at their command — their vote. To this earlier generation of immigrants, to the battle that they waged in defense of their political rights in the 1850s and throughout the century, Panos Dukakis and his generation of newcomers owed a major debt.

SUGGESTED READINGS

Baker, Jean H. *Ambivalent Americans: The Know-Nothing Party in Maryland.* Baltimore: Johns Hopkins University Press, 1977.

Billingon, Ray Allen. *The Protestant Crusade, 1800-1860: The Origins of American Nativism.* Chicago: Quadrangle, 1964 (1938).

Feldberg, Michael. *The Philadelphia Riots of 1844: A Study of Ethnic Conflict.* Westport, Ct.: Greenwood Press, 1975.

Gienapp, William E. *The Origins of the Republican Party 1852-1856.* New York: Oxford University Press, 1987.

Handlin, Oscar. *Boston's Immigrants: A Study in Acculturation.* Cambridge, Mass.: Belknap Press of Harvard University Press, 1979.

Higham, John. *Strangers in the Land.* New York: Atheneum, 1970.

Holt, Michael F. *The Political Crisis of the 1850s.* New York: Wiley, 1978.

Kettner, James H. *The Development of American Citizenship, 1608-1870.* Chapel Hill: University of North Carolina Press, 1978.

Noonan, Carroll John. *Nativism in Connecticut, 1829-1860.* Washington, D.C.: Catholic University of America, 1938.

VOL. XI.—No. 568.] NEW YORK, SATURDAY, NOVEMBER 16, 1867. [SINGLE COPIES TEN CENTS. $4.00 PER YEAR IN ADVANCE.

Entered according to Act of Congress, in the Year 1867, by Harper & Brothers, in the Clerk's Office of the District Court for the Southern District of New York.

"THE FIRST VOTE."—DRAWN BY A. R. WAUD.—[SEE NEXT PAGE.]

This drawing by A. R. Waud, "The First Vote," appeared in *Harper's Weekly* in November 1867. It depicts the extension of voting rights to black men following the Civil War, the first time in U.S. history that black men had been generally recognized as voters. *Source: Museum of American Political Life, University of Hartford.*

4 FROM SLAVERY TO CITIZENSHIP: BLACKS AND THE RIGHT TO VOTE

Eric Foner
Columbia University

In the aftermath of the Civil Rights Movement of the 1950s and 1960s, modern-day Americans regard the principle of "equal treatment before the law" as a basic ideal of our political system. This applies especially to voting rights: Americans today overwhelmingly uphold the idea that participation in the political community by voting should be a guaranteed right for all Americans regardless of race, color, religion, or sex.

Yet, it was not until the mid-nineteenth century that this principle became a central theme of our political life. As Eric Foner explains in the next essay, the American constitutional system was originally founded not on the notion of equal rights, but on the idea of racial exclusion. Not only did the U.S. Constitution as originally ratified in 1788 include subtle protections for the institution of African slavery in the South, he argues, but also during the early-1800s, northern states increasingly restricted free blacks' voting rights at the same time that they widened the franchise for adult white men.

It took a revolutionary event, the American Civil War, Foner contends, to bring blacks into the political system. The war not only brought an end to slavery, but also added two pathbreaking amendments to the Constitution — the Fourteenth Amendment creating the rights of national citizenship, and the Fifteenth Amendment barring restrictions on voting based on race, color, or previous condition of servitude. These amendments, Foner says, were a product of the unusual political atmosphere of the post-Civil War Reconstruction period. By incorporating black Americans — most of them ex-slaves — into the electoral system, the amendments made truly breathtaking changes in American political life.

Yet, the reality of black political rights lasted only as long as the Reconstruction era itself. Though the Fourteenth and Fifteenth Amendments added the principle of equal rights to the text of the Constitution, Foner asserts, federal enforcement of those rights was abandoned at the end of the nineteenth century, to be revived again only with the arrival of the modern Civil Rights struggle. That the rights promised in the Fourteenth and Fifteenth Amendments proved to be so fragile, Foner concludes, shows that each generation of Americans must continue to strive to give them meaning.

The Civil War and Reconstruction produced not simply three constitutional amendments, but a new American constitution. For the Thirteenth, Fourteenth, and Fifteenth Amendments fundamentally redefined the nature of American public life and the rights of the nation's citizens. As a result of the greatest crisis in our country's history, the Constitution was amended first to abolish slavery, then to establish a national citizenship whose rights, enforced by the federal government, were to be enjoyed equally by blacks and whites, and finally to enfranchise the nation's black male population. These were revolutionary changes for a nation whose Constitution, when written in 1787, included clauses that protected the stability of slavery and the political power of slaveholders, and whose laws, from the beginning, were grounded in racism.

When Thomas Jefferson in 1776 proclaimed mankind's inalienable right to life, liberty, and the pursuit of happiness, slavery was already an old institution in America. For well over a century, slaves had tilled the tobacco fields of Virginia and Maryland. Slaves also worked on small farms in parts of the North, and in many artisan shops in cities like New York and Philadelphia. Taking the nation as a whole, one American in five was a black slave when the war for independence began.

During the American Revolution, slavery for the first time became the subject of intense public scrutiny. And the turmoil produced by the war, the implacable logic of revolutionary ideals, and the acts of blacks themselves, all threatened to undermine the institution. With the British offering freedom to slaves who joined the royal cause, tens of thousands fled their owners and gained their liberty. Thousands more escaped bondage by enlisting in the Revolutionary Army. By the early-nineteenth century, every state from Pennsylvania north had taken steps to abolish slavery, either by court decision, constitutional provision, or laws providing for gradual emancipation. Further south, a considerable number of slaveholders, especially in Virginia and Maryland, voluntarily emancipated their slaves. Many others hoped and believed that the institution would soon die out. Nonetheless, the stark fact is that despite manumission, self-emancipation by blacks, and the beginning of abolition in the North, there were more slaves in America at the end of the revolutionary era than at the beginning. The first national census, in 1790, reported that the half-million slave population of 1776 had grown to some 700,000, the vast majority living in the South.

Slavery, moreover, was deeply embedded in the new federal Constitution. Despite widespread condemnation of its inhumanity, the Constitution prohibited the abolition of the African slave trade for twenty years. Every state was required to return fugitives, thereby implicating the entire nation in the system's maintenance. And the Constitution provided that three-fifths of the disfranchised slave population would be counted in determining a state's representation in Congress and its allocation of electoral votes. The three-fifths clause allowed the white South to exert far greater power in national elections than its numbers warranted. Of sixteen presidential elections between 1788 and 1848, all but four placed a southern slaveholder in the White House.

Nonetheless, the Constitution left voting requirements to the individual states, and did nothing to prohibit blacks from exercising the franchise. This was not an issue in the South, where slavery soon entered an era of unprecedented expansion, based on the spread of cotton cultivation. Slaves, of course, were by definition outside of the "political nation," and free blacks were subjected to an increasingly rigid code of laws designed to institutionalize the view that they were a dangerous, unwelcome element of southern life. The question of political rights for any blacks in the South scarcely arose before the Civil War.

The North's black community was far smaller than the South's — on the eve of the Civil War, it numbered only 220,000, or about 1 percent of the region's population. Yet this tiny group was subjected to discrimination in every phase of its life. Racism was not only deeply embedded in the early-nineteenth-century North, but seemed also to become more virulent as the century progressed. Perhaps this was inevitable in a nation whose economic growth depended in large measure on the labor of black slaves, and whose territorial expansion involved the dispossession of one nonwhite people, the Indians, and the conquest of lands inhabited by another, the Mexicans.

Racism affected blacks' economic prospects, since nearly all occupations other than unskilled labor and personal service were barred to them (and even then, their position became increasingly tenuous as large numbers of immigrants flooded the North's labor market beginning in the 1830s). In most northern states, blacks were denied access to public schools, excluded from places of public accommodation and amusement, and prohibited from serving on juries and in state militias. And during the 1840s and 1850s, four northern states — Indiana, Illinois, Iowa, and Oregon — went so far as to prohibit blacks from ever entering their territory.

With regard to the right to vote, northern blacks confronted the same pattern of deteriorating conditions that they faced in other aspects of their lives. In 1800, no northern state restricted the suffrage on the basis of race. Women, of course, were barred from voting, as were men who did not pay taxes or own a specified amount of property. Most black men were poor, but those able to meet the property qualifications could vote alongside whites. But between 1800 and 1860, every free state except Maine that entered the Union, beginning with Ohio in 1803, restricted the suffrage to white males. Moreover, among the older states, even as property qualifications for whites were progressively eliminated, blacks' political rights were more and more constrained. In effect, race (as well as gender) supplanted class as the major line of division between those who could vote and those who could not.

In 1821, the same New York constitutional convention that removed property qualifications for white voters raised the requirement for blacks to $250 — a sum beyond the reach of nearly all black residents of the state. Peter Jay, a delegate who opposed this new provision, eloquently condemned the "unfounded prejudices" that motivated the convention's actions: the arguments against black voting, he declared, "though repeated in various forms, . . . may all be summed up in this: that we are accustomed to look upon black men with contempt — that we will not eat with them — that we will not sit with them — that we will not serve with them in the militia, or on juries, nor in any manner associate with them — and thence it is concluded, that they ought not to vote with us." Sixteen years later, Pennsylvania revoked blacks' right to vote entirely, even though Philadelphia was the home of a black community that included men of education, property, and experience in public affairs. In the 1840s and 1850s, the abolitionist movement struggled to reverse these decisions and to expand blacks' political rights, but to no avail. On the eve of the Civil War, only five northern states, all in New England, allowed blacks to vote on the same terms as whites. In 1857, Chief Justice Roger Taney, in the *Dred Scott* decision, announced that no black person could be a citizen of the United States.

Thus, the principles engrafted onto the Constitution in the amendments of the Civil War era were utterly unprecedented in antebellum America. Not only was the idea of equality before the law for white and black Americans foreign to the political traditions of both North and South, but most Americans looked to the states, not the federal government, to protect the rights of citizens. The greatest threats to liberty, most believed, arose not from the abuse of local authority, but from a too-powerful national state. The Bill of Rights — added to the Constitution in 1791 — reflected this assumption, for it prohibited Congress, but not the states, from abridging citizens' fundamental rights.

An appreciation of how the Civil War amendments changed the Constitution can only be arrived at by looking carefully at the crisis of the 1860s. Two developments during the Civil War were crucial to placing the issue of black citizenship on the national agenda. One was the disintegration of slavery — a process initiated by blacks who abandoned their owners' plantations to head for the lines of the Union army, and given political sanction in the Emancipation Proclamation. The second was the massive enrollment of blacks into the Union armed forces. By the end of the war, some 200,000 black men had served in the army and navy. The "logical result" of black military service, one senator observed in 1864, was that "the black man is henceforth to assume a new status among us."

At the same time, the exigencies of war created a profound alteration in the nature of American government. The need to mobilize the North's resources for modern war produced what one Republican called "a new government," with a greatly expanded income, bureaucracy, and set of responsibilities. And the war inspired a broad nationalism, embraced above all by antislavery reformers, black and white, and Radical Republicans in Congress. With emancipation, these men and women believed, the federal government had become not a threat to local autonomy and individual liberty, but the "custodian of freedom."

The amendments of the 1860s reflected the intersection of these two products of the Civil War — the idea of equality before the law, and the newly empowered national state. The Thirteenth, adopted by Congress in January 1865 and ratified the following fall, not only abolished slavery throughout the Union, but empowered Congress to enforce abolition with "appropriate legislation." Many Republicans believed the amendment authorized Congress to eliminate various kinds of discriminations against blacks as "badges of slavery" that must be swept away along with the South's "peculiar institution."

Most forthright in calling for further action on behalf of blacks' rights were the Radical Republicans, led in the House of Representatives by Thaddeus Stevens of Pennsylvania and in the Senate by Charles Sumner of Massachusetts. The Union's victory in the Civil War, they believed, offered a golden opportunity to purge the nation of "the demon of caste," and to create what Stevens called a "perfect republic" based upon the principle of equality. Some Radicals, like Stevens, went even further, proposing that the national government confiscate lands belonging to the planter class and distribute it among the former slaves. Most Republicans were unwilling to go this far, but they did insist that blacks should enjoy the same opportunity as whites to compete for advancement in the economic marketplace.

When Congress reconvened in December 1865, the Radicals represented only a minority among Republicans. But events quickly pushed the more numerous moderates in their direction. President

Abraham Lincoln had been succeeded in office by Andrew Johnson of Tennessee in April 1865. During the summer and fall of 1865, Johnson had initiated his own program of Reconstruction, which in effect placed the old planter class back in control of southern affairs. Southern public life was restricted entirely to whites, and the new state governments sought to establish a labor system as close to slavery as possible. Blacks were required by law to sign yearly labor contracts; refusal to do so, or attempting to leave work before a contract expired, meant arrest, a prison term, or being leased out to anyone who would pay the culprit's fine. No such regulations applied to white citizens.

These laws, known as the Black Codes, seemed to the North to make a mockery of emancipation. In response, Congress in the spring of 1866 enacted the Civil Rights Act, which became law over Johnson's veto. This defined all persons born in the United States (except Indians) as national citizens, and spelled out rights they were to enjoy equally without regard to race — including making contracts, bringing lawsuits, owning property, and receiving equal treatment before the courts. No state could deprive an individual of these basic rights; if they did so, state officials would be held accountable in federal court.

In constitutional terms, the Civil Rights Act of 1866 represented the first attempt to give meaning to the Thirteenth Amendment, to define the consequences of emancipation. If states could deny blacks the right to choose their employment, seek better jobs, and enforce payment of wages, noted one congressman, "then I demand to know, of what practical value is the amendment abolishing slavery?" The first statutory definition of American citizenship, the Civil Rights Act embodied a profound change in federal-state relations. The underlying assumption — that the federal government possessed the power to define and protect citizens' rights — was a striking departure in American law.

One of the purposes of the Fourteenth Amendment, approved by Congress in June 1866, was to prevent a future Congress from repealing the guarantees in the Civil Rights Act. But the amendment's purposes were far broader than this. Its heart was the first section, which declared all persons born or naturalized in the United States to be both national and state citizens, and which prohibited the states from abridging citizens' "privileges and immunities," depriving any person of life, liberty, or property without "due process of law," or denying them "equal protection of the laws."

For more than a century, politicians, judges, lawyers, and scholars have debated the meaning of these elusive terms. The problem of ascertaining the amendment's "original intent" is compounded by the fact that its language was a compromise with which no one seemed "entirely satisfied." Yet despite many drafts, deletions, and changes, its central principle remained constant: a national guarantee of equality before the law. This was now so widely accepted in Republican circles, and had already been so fully discussed, that compared with now-forgotten clauses concerning representation in Congress, the Confederate debt, and the disqualification of certain Confederates from office, the first section inspired relatively little debate. It was "so just," one Congressman declared, "that no member of this House can seriously object to it."

If the Civil Rights Act listed numerous specific rights a state could not abridge, the Fourteenth Amendment used only the broadest language. Unlike a statute, it was intended as a statement of principle. Both Radical Republicans and moderates preferred to allow Congress and the federal courts maximum flexibility in combatting the multitude of injustices confronting southern blacks.

Transcending boundaries of race and region, the Fourteenth Amendment changed and broadened the definition of freedom for all Americans, for its language challenged legal discrimination throughout the nation. Nonetheless, many reformers were deeply disappointed with the amendment. Republicans in 1866 were divided on the question of black suffrage. The amendment did not grant blacks the vote — it merely threatened to reduce Southern representation in Congress if blacks continued to be denied the franchise. And, in its representation clause, the amendment for the first time introduced the word "male" into the Constitution. Suffrage restrictions that reduced the number of male voters would cost a state representation; women could continue to be barred from voting without penalty. The result was a split between advocates of blacks' rights and women's rights.

Ideologically and politically, nineteenth-century feminism had been tied to abolition. During the war, the organized women's movement had put aside the suffrage issue to join in the crusade for the Union and emancipation. Now, leaders like Elizabeth Cady Stanton and Susan B. Anthony insisted that if the Constitution were to be changed, the claims of women must not be ignored. To Radicals and abolitionists who insisted that this was "the Negro's hour," feminists defined it, instead, as the hour for change, an opportunity that must be seized or another generation might pass "ere the constitutional door will again be opened." To which Radicals, even those sympathetic to the idea of women's suffrage, insisted that tying the issues of black rights and women's suffrage would doom both to defeat. A Civil War had not been fought over the status of women, nor had thirty years of prior agitation awaked public consciousness on the issue.

Repudiated by the southern states and President Johnson, the Fourteenth Amendment became the centerpiece of the congressional campaign in 1866. When Republicans swept the fall elections, they moved not only to ensure the amendment's ratification, but granted the right to vote to black men in the South and mandated the formation of new southern governments resting on manhood suffrage. Mainstream Republicans had become convinced that this was the only way of empowering blacks to protect their newly acquired freedom, and ensuring that "loyal" men assumed control of government in the South.

The coming of black suffrage, although confined at this point to the South, marked a radical departure in American history, one that can only be explained by the momentous crisis of the 1860s. In America, the ballot did more than identify who could vote — it defined a collective national identity (as women's suffrage advocates so tirelessly pointed out). Democrats had fought black suffrage on precisely these grounds. "Without reference to the question of equality," declared Indiana Senator Thomas Hendricks, "I say we are not of the same race; we are so different that we ought not to compose one political community." The enfranchisement of blacks marked a powerful repudiation of such thinking.

Under this policy of Radical Reconstruction, interracial democracy flourished for several years throughout the South, and blacks probably exercised more genuine political power than at any time in our history, before or since. Between 1867, when black men in the former Confederate states were enfranchised, and 1877, when the last Reconstruction governments were overthrown, hundreds of blacks, the majority of them former slaves, served in positions ranging from governor (briefly) of Louisiana, to congressman, legislator, sheriff, justice of the peace, and school board official. The Republican party became an institution as central to the black community as the school and church. When not deterred by violence, blacks eagerly attended political gatherings and voted in extraordinary numbers; their turnout sometimes approached 90 percent. "It is the hardest thing in the world to keep a Negro away from the polls," commented a white Alabaman. "That is the one thing he will do, to vote." However inadequate as a response to the legacy of slavery (since Reconstruction failed to address the economic plight of the former slaves), it remains a tragedy that the lofty goals of civil and political equality were not permanently achieved. And long after they had been stripped of the franchise, blacks would recall the act of voting as a defiance of inherited norms of white supremacy, and regard "the loss of suffrage as being the loss of freedom."

In 1869, Congress approved the last of the postwar amendments, the Fifteenth, which prohibited the federal or state governments from depriving individuals of the vote on racial grounds. For the first time, black voting came to the entire nation, North as well as South. But the amendment's narrow, negative language was a far cry from the broad statement of principle embodied in the Fourteenth. Radicals had desired an amendment that made suffrage requirements "uniform throughout the land." Yet in 1869, the Northern states wished to retain their own restrictions on the suffrage. In the West, the Chinese could not vote. Pennsylvania demanded the payment of state taxes; Rhode Island still had a property qualification. A positive amendment enfranchising, say, all adult males at age twenty-one, would alienate northern Republicans who wished to retain such restrictions. Indeed, in a reversal of long-established political traditions, support for black voting now seemed less controversial than efforts to combat other forms of inequality. By allowing states to continue to bar women from the polls, the amendment further angered feminist leaders. Moreover, its language left open the possibility of poll taxes, literacy tests, and other ostensibly nonracial requirements that could, and would, be used to disfranchise the vast majority of southern black men.

With the end of Reconstruction in 1877, the egalitarian impulse embodied in the amendments of the 1860s faded from national life. The Thirteenth, Fourteenth, and Fifteenth Amendments remained parts of the Constitution, but as far as blacks were concerned, they increasingly became dead letters. Even in the early 1870s, the Supreme Court had begun to restrict the rights protected under the Fourteenth Amendment. After 1877, the federal courts employed their expanded powers under the Fourteenth Amendment primarily to protect corporations from local regulation (on the grounds that corporations were "persons" who could not be deprived of their property rights by state agencies). By 1896, in *Plessy* v. *Ferguson*, the Court found racial segregation mandated by state law perfectly compatible with the doctrine of equality before the law. And it did nothing when, in the 1890s and early- twentieth century, one southern state after another stripped black citizens of the right to vote.

Only in our own time did a great political reform movement and a socially conscious Supreme Court again breathe life into the racial egalitarianism, and the broad view of national responsibility for citizens' rights , that form the essence of the postwar amendments. One landmark of the "second Reconstruction" of our own time was the Voting Rights Act of 1965, which effectively reenfranchised blacks in the southern states. Today, blacks vote in roughly the same proportion as whites, and hold office as mayors of many of our largest cities. Yet the history of the postwar amendments and the right to vote underscores how fragile individual rights can be, even when protected by the letter of the Constitution, and how each generation must strive to give new meaning to the ideals of liberty and equality.

SUGGESTED READINGS

Berlin, Ira, and Ronald Hoffman, eds., *Slavery and Freedom in the Age of the American Revolution.* Charlottesville: U.S. Capitol Historical Society by the University Press of Virginia, 1983.

Davis, David Brion. *The Problem of Slavery in the Age of Revolution.* Ithaca, N.Y.: Cornell University Press, 1975.

Harding, Vincent. *There is a River: The Black Struggle for Freedom in America.* New York: Harcourt Brace Jovanovich, 1981.

Litwack, Leon. *North of Slavery: The Negro in the Free States.* Chicago: University of Chicago Press, 1961.

Frederickson, George M. *The Black Image in the White Mind: The Debate on Afro-American Character and Destiny, 1817-1914.* New York: Harper & Row, 1971.

Foner, Eric. *Reconstruction: America's Unfinished Revolution.* New York: Harper & Row, 1988.

Wood engraving from *Frank Leslie's Weekly*, February 1871, depicting the appearance of Victoria Woodhull before the Judiciary Committee of the U.S. House of Representatives to advocate women's voting rights, a radical idea at that time. Behind Woodhull sits Elizabeth Cady Stanton, who inaugurated the American women's suffrage movement in 1848. *Source: Museum of American Political Life, University of Hartford.*

5 TAKING LAW INTO THEIR OWN HANDS: VOTING WOMEN DURING RECONSTRUCTION

Ellen Carol DuBois
University of California at Los Angeles

Until the late-nineteenth century, the main prospect in life for white American women was marriage and family. Although some young, unmarried women worked in textile mills and others took on the "female" employments of school teaching or domestic service, the chief occupation of the vast majority of American women was to be wife, mother, and homemaker.

Laws and social custom reinforced women's confinement to the "domestic sphere." Until the mid-1800s, married women could not own or convey property. Until the late-1800s, they were barred from the professions, such as medicine or law. And of course, until the early-1900s, they could not vote or hold public office. These restrictions were usually justified with the argument that women were of a different nature than men, that their power to bear children made them more suitable for domestic life and religious affairs than for the rough-and-tumble world of politics. And so, except for a short period in the early years of the nineteenth century in New Jersey, and in a few western states at the end of the nineteenth century, women were largely excluded from public life until the Nineteenth Amendment granted them the vote in 1920.

Despite the prevailing conviction that women belonged with home and family, the seeds for their eventual entry into public life were planted in the mid-1800s. In the essay which follows, Ellen Carol DuBois argues that the mid-nineteenth-century movement to abolish slavery and the post-Civil War amendments designed to guarantee blacks their political rights both contributed to founding America's women's suffrage movement (called "woman suffrage" during the nineteenth century). Having failed to secure explicit guarantees for woman suffrage in the post-Civil War amendments, DuBois contends, suffragists drew from the Fourteenth Amendment's idea of "national citizenship" to justify the vote for women. And even though late-nineteenth-century suffragists failed to establish their voting rights in this way, she advises us, the militance and devotion with which they pursued that cause is a reminder to voters in the late-twentieth century that the right to vote ought to be taken seriously.

It is difficult to undertake an essay on voting, even a historical one, without being acutely aware of the disrepute into which voting has fallen. Nowadays, voting is widely regarded as a minor political gesture, a patriotic ritual that is encouraged precisely because it signifies nothing. The following history of nineteenth-century women's efforts to win the vote is a reminder that this was not always the case. The woman suffragists of the 1870s regarded the right to vote with passionate devotion and fought for it with great militancy. They were defeated in their drive for the vote, but there is something to learn from historical efforts that were failures as well as from those that were successful. There is buried in this history of women demanding to vote a lost vision of the purposes to which government can be put, a sense of the positive relationship between popular power and the political process which remains relevant today, maybe relevant enough to revive our faith in voting.

We also take voting women for granted today. Yet, there are hints that women approach voting somewhat differently than men, reflecting our harder struggle to get the vote. Increasingly in the last decade a "gender gap" has emerged in voting patterns, reflected by a growing tendency for women to vote more Democratic, more in favor of social spending, more against militarism. Such differences are the result, not of some inherent moral divergence in the sexes, but of women's changing social circumstances, especially in the labor force. The gender gap also reflects the revival of a political movement — feminism — that has moved women's politics in a liberal direction. When the League of Women Voters abandoned its sponsorship of the second presidential debate in the 1988 campaign, vigorously indicting the hypocrisy of the entire campaign, it was drawing on its historical roots in the suffrage movement and reminding us of a long feminist tradition of believing in voting as an act of popular democracy.

Although the women's rights tradition in the United States reaches back to the era of the French Revolution, the demand for equal political rights for women was not articulated until the 1840s. While early feminists demanded economic rights and intellectual equality, the widespread conviction about women's fundamentally domestic nature kept them from insisting that women were men's equals in political life, or from imagining women voting, the ultimate public act.

The pioneer visionary of the movement for woman suffrage — the first feminist to make the demand for women's votes — was Elizabeth Cady Stanton, who came from the abolitionist movement, the radical northern movement advocating the immediate abolition of African slavery. Most abolitionists dismissed politics entirely, regarding the

Constitution as irredeemably pro-slavery and political parties as allies of the slaveholding class. Abolitionist leader William Lloyd Garrison was famous for declaring that, in a country that protected slaveholding, voting was a sin. Eventually, the abolitionist movement began to develop a more pragmatic approach to politics, a recognition that although corruption and cowardice were all inevitable aspects of politics, still political action was the inescapable route for social change. This was Elizabeth Stanton's milieu. Like other politically minded abolitionists, she regarded politics as participation, not in the corruption of the power of the state, but in the struggle over who will control it.

Under Elizabeth Stanton's leadership, and that of the indefatigable organizer who became her partner in 1851, Susan B. Anthony, a women's rights movement began slowly to attract other adherents. In towns throughout New England and the Midwest, a few individuals became identified as the local strong-minded women. Perhaps they collected signatures on a petition to the state legislature or journeyed to hear a traveling speaker and came back to tell their neighbors. The establishment of economic rights for married women was the topic that principally concerned them, and growing pressure from organized groups of women persuaded legislators to pass married women's property laws. As for woman suffrage, it was the crowning jewel of women's rights, but it remained an abstraction until the Civil War.

The real breakthrough for the woman suffrage movement came with the abolition of slavery during the Civil War, and the Constitutional amendments that followed it. The Thirteenth Amendment, which wrote abolition into the Constitution, did not address political equality explicitly, but raised the issue implicitly. First of all, the very fact that slavery could be obliterated by constitutional act greatly expanded respect for the power of politics to make significant change and for the capacity of popular movements to alter the terms of politics. More concretely, the question of voting rights for blacks followed immediately upon the fact of their emancipation: if black people were not slaves, were they not citizens; and if citizens, were they not voters?

The richest fruits of the demand for black suffrage were the Fourteenth and Fifteenth Amendments, ratified in 1868 and 1870, respectively. The first section of the Fourteenth Amendment was intended to repudiate the 1857 Supreme Court decision of *Dred Scott* v. *Sandford* that declared that blacks were not citizens. The amendment offers a grand statement of national citizenship, which is extended not to races or genders, but to "all persons born or naturalized in the United States." Nor are the rights of national citizens explicitly enumerated; instead the amendment concentrates on extending them to all persons and protecting them from infringement. This lack of particulars has at times been used by the courts to limit the scope of the Fourteenth Amendment, but the very vagueness of the first section's generalities also makes it one of the most important, potentially powerful and frequently contested elements of the Constitution with respect to equal rights.

Voting rights do come up explicitly in the Fourteenth Amendment's second section. This section begins to establish the right of ex-slaves to vote, but through the back door. Not yet willing to declare a federal right to vote, the amendment's framers devised penalties for states which deprived freedmen of their voting rights, the proportional reduction of their Congressional delegation. Two years later, the ratification of the Fifteenth Amendment finally extended constitutional protection of the right to vote to freedmen.

But what about the political rights of women in all this? While the Fourteenth Amendment was being formulated in 1866, women's rights leaders submitted thousands of signatures to Congress to see that the Fourteenth Amendment recognized their longstanding claim to political rights and was truly democratic in its provisions. "The undersigned earnestly but respectfully request that in any change or amendment of the Constitution you may propose to extend or regulate suffrage there shall be no distinctions made between men and women."[1] But the process of compromise which forged the Fourteenth Amendment left no room for women's votes. To the horror of women's rights leaders, the second section of the amendment, the one that addressed voting explicitly, used the term "male citizens" to designate the body of voters whose representation would be reduced in case southern states disfranchised blacks. In other words, the amendment made reference to sex only to exclude women.

The first reaction of the most militant advocates of woman suffrage to the Fourteenth Amendment was to condemn it for establishing "an aristocracy of sex." They also objected to the Fifteenth Amendment when it was passed by Congress in 1869 for not listing sex along with race, color, and previous condition of servitude as a prohibited means of disfranchisement. Feminists tried to persuade Congress to draft an additional constitutional amendment to enfranchise women. But without the historic link with black suffrage, they were powerless.

Then, in 1869, woman suffrage leaders took a radical turn in their attitude to the Fourteenth Amendment. Instead of focusing on the exclusions of the second section, they began to emphasize the grand, if vague, inclusions of the first section. This more positive interpretation of the Fourteenth Amendment was known as the New Departure. The argument was that the Constitution as amended, especially the Fourteenth Amendment when properly interpreted, already protected women in their right to vote. Put simply, no additional amendment was necessary. The New Departure's constitutional specifics were actually quite simple. Its first premise was that the first section of the Fourteenth Amendment established the universality of national citizenship and the obligation of the federal government to protect all citizens in the "privileges and immunities" of citizenship. Its second point was that women, as "persons," were equally citizens with men. Its third assertion — the one most obvious to New Departure activists but most troubling to the courts — was that voting was one of the "privileges and immunities of citizenship," the chief jewel of citizenship.

The argument that women were already enfranchised was first formally made by a St. Louis married couple, Francis and Virginia Minor, in 1869. However, the New Departure was not only a lawyer's exercise, but was also a constitutional distillation of a widely held political faith about the nature of political rights and the importance of democratic politics. The argument that voting was already women's right, that women had only to seize that which was theirs, that the role of the Constitution was to defend rights rather than bestow them, made considerable popular sense to women in the post-Civil War Reconstruction era. New Departure activists literally acted out their right to vote: they went to the polls and submitted their names to the registrars and their votes to the polling officials. Sometimes they actually succeeded in casting their votes; sometimes registrars refused them But in all cases, women's direct action voting was tremendously inspiring and significantly increased the number of women willing to identify with the idea of votes for women.

The fact that the first examples of women's direct action voting occurred even before the Minors' formal constitutional exposition, strongly suggests that the New Departure argument flowed from a genuinely popular attitude toward voting, democracy and political power. In 1868, in Vineland New Jersey, almost two hundred women, including at least one black woman, cast their votes into a separate ballot box and then tried to get election officials to include them with the men's votes. Stanton and Anthony's newspaper *The Revolution* reported that, at an election day celebration, "the platform was crowded with earnest refined intellectual women, who feel it was good for them to be there. One beautiful girl said 'I feel so much stronger for having voted.'"[2] The women of Vineland repeated their efforts and the ballot box eventually became an icon; in the Vineland historical society, the curator will still get it out of a cabinet and show it to you. From Vineland, the idea of women voting spread to nearby towns. In Roseville, New Jersey, veteran feminist Lucy Stone and her mother tried — but failed — to register their votes. We can imagine that the ambition to vote had been growing in her for the two decades she had been speaking for women's rights.

At the other end of the continent, in Washington Territory, Mary Olney Brown also decided that she had a right to vote. The idea first occurred to her in 1867 and she wrote to "some of the prominent women of the towns but . . . I was looked upon as a fanatic and the idea of a woman voting was regarded as an absurdity." "Many women wished to vote," she believed. "They knew it was the only way to secure their rights and yet they had not the courage to go to the polls in defiance of custom." Finally, in 1869, she announced that she would go with her daughter, husband and son-in-law to vote. Newspapers around the state predicted that she would "unsex herself by dabbling in the filthy pool of politics." At the polling place, she declared to election officials that " I [am] an American citizen, and a native-born citizen at that; and I wish to show you from the four-teenth amendment to the Constitution of the United States, that women are citizens having the constitutional right to vote."

In her account Brown described how these local politicians refused to accept her vote, on the grounds that "the laws of Congress don't extend over Washington territory." Their ignorance contrasted so profoundly with Brown's own confident constitutionalism that "a look of disgust and shame was depicted on nearly every countenance and the cause of woman suffrage had advanced perceptibly in the minds of the audience." The next year when Brown was again refused the right to vote, she watched as a male citizen, who was drunk, was brought to the polling place in a wagon by his fellows to vote. She protested in as constitutionally dignified a language as she could. "The law gives women the right to vote in this territory and you three men who have been appointed to receive our votes sit here and arbitrarily refused to take them, giving no reason why. . . . There is no law to sustain you in this usurpation of power."[3]

News of the efforts of women to register and vote spread. Women's rights and mainstream journals reported on their activities, but infor-mation was also passed by word of mouth. Many sisters or friends, often in different towns or states, tried to vote. One woman might get her vote accepted, while her friend or kinswoman would have a different experience. Mary Olney Brown includes the story of her sister who was inspired to try to vote in a nearby town. Brown's sis-ter was more successful. She and her friends prepared a special picnic feast for the election officials. "When the voting was resumed, the women, my sister being the first, handed in their ballots as if they had always been accustomed to voting. . . . One lady, seventy-two years old, said she thanked the Lord that he had let her live until she could vote. She had often prayed to see the day and now she was proud to cast her first ballot."

Women voted in the East, in the Midwest and in the far West; there is one piece of evidence of black freedwomen in South Carolina voting. Voting accelerated in 1870 and 1871 and peaked during the crucial presidential year of 1872. Evidence exists of hundreds trying to vote and most likely there were more. Most of these women were not prominent outside of their own towns.

One of the most striking things about the women who voted during the Radical Reconstruction era of the 1870s is the collective nature of their direct action. Today, we experience voting as a private, even isolating act. Although the premise of our voting is popular democracy — the people rule — voting often impresses us with the powerlessness of our individual ballots. Certainly, these women believed in the right to vote as an individual right; this made their aspiration to vote a feminist one. But individual rights were to be achieved and experienced collectively. The voting women of the 1870s always went to the polls in groups. Some were married, some single, some taxpayers, some not, most were white, a few were black. Typically, one woman, already a suffrage activist, organized her friends and relatives to join her in her protest. Susan B. Anthony started with her sister and cousins and eventually got fifty other women to join her at the polls in Rochester; so did Sara Spencer in Washington, D.C., Carrie Burnham in Philadelphia, and the aging Grimke Sisters in Hyde Park, Massachusetts. In Bridgeport, Connecticut, Anna Middlebrook organized nineteen women to join her at the polls.

Appearing at the polls in groups undoubtedly gave women's efforts to vote greater force, and it demonstrated that although political rights are individual, political power is collective. Another way to say the same thing is that although these women claimed their right to vote as individuals, independent of sex, they intended to exercise that right as women, conscious of their difference from men. Men surrounded their voting with the emblems of their traditional, masculine political culture — torchlight parades on election eve, boisterous male conviviality on election day. These women used the small details of their womanly lives to indicate how they felt about voting. Nanette Gardner, who successfully voted in Detroit in 1871, "presented herself at the polls with a vase of flowers and also a prepared ballot, which she had decorated. . . ." She prepared a beautiful hand-sewn "banner of white satin, trimmed with gold fringe" to present to the election official who received her vote; on it she embroidered "to Peter Hill, Alderman of the Ninth Ward . . . by recognizing civil liberty and equality for women, he has placed the last and brightest jewel on the brow of Michigan."[4]

Underlying voting women's confidence and sense of entitlement was a radical ideology about equal rights and political power that they shared with other visionaries of the Reconstruction era. Three important elements of this radicalism were: a popular sovereignty theory of the sources of political power which treated voting as a natural right; an egalitarian belief in the absolute universality of individual rights; and, a new, more positive sense of the power of the federal government, which regarded it as the friend, not the enemy, of rights. These Reconstruction era convictions represent a distinctive vision of the purposes of government, which subsequently disappeared, but that still has something to teach us about the possibilities of democratic politics.

Nothing was so basic to the actions of Reconstruction era voting women as the conviction that the right to vote was inherent, not bestowed. When Carrie Burnham presented herself to a Philadelphia registrar, she declared that her actions were based on the principle that suffrage was an absolute right, not "a gift of society"; for, as she told the election official, "the theory of the right to the franchise as a gift bore with it the power to restrict [even] the male citizen's suffrage and to strike at the principle of self government." Stanton also thought that the notion that suffrage was a privilege, granted by government according to its own standards of order and probity was patently "untenable and anti-republican." Rather, "suffrage is a natural right — as necessary to man under government, for the protection of person and property, as are air and motion to life." From this perspective, the people's rights preceded and authorized government, not the other way around.[5]

Lest this sound no different than eighteenth century notions of the consent of the governed, it is important to proceed to the second distinguishing element of Reconstruction radicalism — its aggressive egalitarianism. The New Departure claim was that political rights inhered universally; it was the task of the Reconstruction generation to secure the rights of "proud white men" for those who had historically been deprived of them — blacks and women. The emphasis was not so much on individual rights as on equal rights, especially for the lowly. While earlier criticisms of the Fourteenth Amendment had inclined woman suffragists to oppose their interests to those of black men, this perspective encouraged them to identify themselves with ex-slaves, for both groups were seeking emancipation from tyranny into the full enjoyment of freedom. Another way to make this point is to say that underlying the actions of voting women was the implication that the fundamental constitutional right of national citizenship was the universal right not to be discriminated against.

The third element underlying the thought of the New Departure women was a positive equation between federal power and the aggressive realization of equal rights, what we might call an implicit theory of affirmative action. Traditional understandings regarded the national government as the potential enemy of rights; the Bill of Rights protects various rights solely by enjoining the federal government from infringing on them. But the Fourteenth Amendment reversed the order; it relied on federal power to protect citizens against the actions of the states. In our own time, suspicion of federal power in the name of the people's rights has been revived and renamed Reaganism; but this stance makes far more sense for "proud white men," than for those who do not yet enjoy all the rights to which they are entitled. The perspective of women who voted during the Reconstruction era was derived from that of the ex-slaves. The women believed that federal power could play an affirmative role in realizing equal rights. Stanton particularly believed in this equation between federal power and equal rights; the way she expressed it was that only the national government had the power to "homogenize" rights; obligated to act with an even hand, the federal government raised the lowly to make them the equal of the high born.[6]

In just this spirit of aggressive federal action on behalf of voting rights, Congress passed the Enforcement Acts in 1870 and 1871 to enforce the civil and political rights of the freedmen. Essentially the first voting rights legislation, the Enforcement Acts dictated financial penalties for state election officials who interfered with the constitutional rights of citizens to vote, and authorized the use of federal courts to enable thwarted voters to sue. The acts were intended to protect the freedmen against the recalcitrance of southern states with no intention of protecting freemen's rights; but voting women saw in the legislation an opportunity to bring federal power to bear on behalf of their own rights. Claiming that the acts applied to them, women who were not allowed to register and/or vote began to bring suits against election officials. By 1872 several major women's rights cases were working their way up through the federal courts to test the meaning of the Constitution and the intent of the federal government to realize political equality. It is to these cases that we now turn to see the fate of the New Departure.

While voting women brought their cases before the courts with great optimism, expecting their interpretations to be vindicated, they were uniformly defeated. The courts did not object so much to the women's rights part of the New Departure argument — that women had the same rights as men — as they did to the fundamental democratic assertion, that political rights were universal and originated in the people. It was, in other words, the constitutional legitimacy of their natural rights theory of political equality that the voting women of Reconstruction sought to establish and on which the historical significance of their actions rests.

In Washington, D.C., in 1871, Sara Spencer and seventy other voting women sued election officials for refusing to permit them to vote. District male citizens had been awarded the vote in the aftermath of the Civil War, and there, Spencer reasoned, questions of federal authority over political rights could be tested without the added complication of state sovereignty. Judge Cartter ruled against the D.C. women voters. He conceded that the Fourteenth Amendment included women with men in the privileges and immunities of national citizenship. What he rejected was the egalitarian theory of suffrage on which the case rested. To concede that voting was a right of citizenship would "involve the destruction of civil government. The right of all men to vote is as fully recognized in the population of our large centers and cities as can well be done. The result is political profligacy and violence verging upon anarchy."[7]

Susan B. Anthony also argued that the Constitution already enfranchised women before the court, but her case was different. She did not institute a civil suit against election officials but was arrested on federal criminal charges for illegal voting a few weeks after the 1872 election. Anthony was the most famous suffragist in the nation, and her arrest must have been authorized at the highest level. The outcome of Anthony's trial further demonstrated that the federal government was determined to put an end to the popular constitutionalism that animated the New Departure women. In the courtroom, Anthony delivered a long, passionate defense of her actions. The judge, a recent appointee to the Supreme Court, then took the extraordinary step of directing the jury to find a verdict of guilty, which they did. Anthony was prohibited from appealing her case or even from going to jail to protest her verdict. Inasmuch as the point of her arrest was to sever Constitutional interpretation and popular activism, the activist Anthony would not be the one allowed to appear before the courts to assert women's claims.

The New Departure argument finally reached the U.S. Supreme Court in 1875 with Virginia Minor's case. The crux of the Minor case was the contention that voting was a right of national citizenship, which women, along with men, enjoyed. To the Minors, this claim was so obvious, so basic to the entire meaning of Reconstruction, as to be barely in need of argument. "We claim, and presume it will not be disputed, that the elective franchise is a privilege of citizenship within the meaning of the Constitution." Again, the Court did not linger over the claim that women were citizens. Rather it ruled that voting was not a right of citizenship, but a privilege bestowed by government so long as it did not disrupt social and political order. Unanimously it ruled that "the Constitution of the United States does not confer the right of suffrage upon any one." The court was clearly preparing its retreat from any commitment even to black suffrage. Susan B. Anthony understood this. "If we once establish the false principle that United States citizenship does not carry with it the right to vote in every state in this Union," she predicted, "there is no end to the petty freaks and cunning devices that will be resorted to exclude one and another class of citizens from the right of suffrage." Soon the Court began to rule that the amendments were too narrow even in cases explicitly involving black men, and the age of de facto disfranchisement had begun.[8]

What legacy did the voting women of the 1870s leave? With the Court's negative ruling in the Minor case, the woman suffrage movement shifted its strategy from direct action to constitutional amendment and the slow work of popular education. This is the route it pursued until 1920, when the Nineteenth Amendment was ratified, although throughout those years one and another suffragist would see possibilities in the existing provisions of the Constitution and propose some clever legal mechanism for exploiting them. Nor did the impulse behind direct action voting entirely die away; early in the twentieth century, women, anxious to participate politically and exasperated with their disfranchisement, engaged in mock voting in large numbers, and publicized the results to try to lend them real power. The deepest mark of the New Departure was to make women's rights and political equality indelibly constitutional issues. As historian Norma Basch has written of the Minor case, "it drew the inferiority of women's status out of the grooves of common law assumptions and state provisions and thrust it into the maelstrom of constitutional conflict. The demand for woman suffrage . . . acquired a contentious national life."[9]

As for the underlying philosophy of political power and equal rights which, I have argued, motivated and inspired these women: these possibilities still await us in the Reconstruction amendments.

One of the ironies of our recent constitutional bicentennial, which was intended to solidify a conservative history of the U.S. Constitution, has been to alert scholars to the history of great battles over the meaning of the Constitution in this era and at other times. Such notions — the identification of popular sovereignty and federal power, the equation of aggressive egalitarianism with constitutional authority — are not so much in evidence these days; but these are the very ideas that make political rights worth fighting for and wielding. Perhaps that is the greatest message that this episode in the history of woman suffrage has for us today.

NOTES

1. Elizabeth Cady Stanton, "Gerrit Smith on Petitions," *The Revolution,* January 14, 1869, 24-25.

2. Cited in Eleanor Flexner, *Century of Struggle: The Women's Rights Movement in the United States* (New York, 1959), 165.

3. Elizabeth Cady Stanton, Susan B. Anthony and Matilda Joslyn Gage, eds., *History of Woman Suffrage,* vol. III: *1876-1885* (Rochester, 1886), 780-786.

4. Ibid., III: 523.

5. Ibid., III: 600-1; II: 185.

6. Ibid., II: 80-92.

7. Ibid., II: 597-599.

8. *Minor* v. *Happersett.* 21 Wallace 162 (1875) quoted in Stanton, Anthony, and Gage, eds., *History of Woman Suffrage,* II: 717-41; *History of Woman Suffrage,* II: 675-79.

9. Norma Basch, "The Minor Case," Paper delivered at Women and the Constitution Conference, American University, Washington, D.C., April 1988.

SUGGESTED READINGS

Baer, Judith. *Equality Under the Constitution: Reclaiming the Four-teenth Amendment.* Ithaca: Cornell University Press, 1983.

Buhle, Mari Jo, and Paul Buhle, eds. *The Concise History of Woman Suffrage.* Urbana: University of Illinois Press, 1978.

DuBois, Ellen Carol. *Feminism and Suffrage: The Emergence of an Independent Women's Movement in America, 1848-1869.* Ithaca: Cornell University Press, 1978.

_____, ed. *Elizabeth Cady Stanton, Susan B. Anthony: Correspondence, Writings, Speeches.* New York: Schocken, 1981.

_____. "Outgrowing the Compact of the Fathers: Equal Rights, Woman Suffrage and the United States Constitu-tion, 1820-1878." *Journal of American History* 74 (December 1987), 836-62.

Flexner, Eleanor. *Century of Struggle: The Women's Rights Movement in the United States.* Revised. Cambridge, Mass.: Belknap Press of Harvard University Press, 1975.

Noun, Louise. *Strong Minded Women: The Emergence of the Woman Suffrage Movement in Iowa.* Ames: University of Iowa Press, 1969.

Selected political buttons from the 1970s and 1980s proclaiming women voters' potential force in politics. The buttons reflect an important theme of women's politics since the 1920s, the idea that women can secure governmental action in regard to social reform and women's issues by voting as a bloc. *Source: Museum of American Political Life, University of Hartford.*

6 CONSTITUTIONAL POLITICS AND THE FEMINIST MOVEMENT†

Mary Fainsod Katzenstein
Cornell University

The tradition of women's rights in American history is now a century-and-one-half old. Beginning with the first women's rights convention at the small farming village of Seneca Falls, New York, in 1848, women campaigned to improve their social status through changes in the law regarding women's property rights, their right to serve on juries, their right to equal and full employment opportunities, and other matters. But at the center of the women's movement in the twentieth century were the organized campaigns to secure amendments to the U. S. Constitution — an amendment providing for women's right to vote and an amendment guaranteeing them equal rights.

The campaign for suffrage lasted nearly a century. First proposed at the Seneca Falls Convention by Elizabeth Cady Stanton in 1848, the vote was the focus for women's activism during the Civil War era, during the period of non-progress in the late-1800s that activists called the "doldrums," and during the final phase of mobilization that led to ratification during the second decade of the twentieth century. To the great joy of women's rights activists, the Nineteenth Amendment was formally ratified as part of the U.S. Constitution in August 1920.

The campaign for an Equal Rights Amendment (ERA) has lasted nearly as long. Introduced in 1923 by militant suffragists such as Alice Paul who organized the National Women's Party in the aftermath of the suffrage victory, the amendment simply stated that "Men and women shall have equal rights throughout the United States and every place subject to its jurisdiction." Despite its simplicity, the ERA met little success during the 1920s, was forgotten during the Great Depression and World War II, but was revived as a major goal of the modern women's movement during the 1970s. Although Congress extended the ratification deadline for the ERA from 1979 to 1982, it fell three states short of the necessary three-fourths majority, and thus did not become part of the Constitution.

Women's rights activists of the 1920s regarded the suffrage amendment as a great victory, just as modern activists regard the downfall of

†The author thanks Uday Singh Mehta for his suggestions on an earlier draft of this essay.

the ERA as a great defeat. But in retrospect, modern observers wonder what the two movements for constitutional change really accomplished for women. Did acquiring the right to vote really change women's place in public life? Did it empower women, allowing them to make important changes in public policy, especially in regard to women's issues? Moreover, has the failure of the ERA to secure ratification meant that modern women are powerless to secure their equal rights? In sum, what long-term impact did these important campaigns for constitutional change have on women's status in society? In the essay that follows, Mary Fainsod Katzenstein argues that the very act of mobilizing to change women's constitutional rights dramatically enlarged women's role in public life and improved their status in society. The struggle to secure constitutional change, she maintains, was as important as constitutional changes themselves.

The bicentennial celebration of the Constitution invokes within each of us, I suspect, a repertoire of different responses, some celebratory, some circumspect. On the side of circumspection is the fact that when the Founding Fathers used the phrase, "We the people," they did not, as Justice Thurgood Marshall reminds us, "have in mind the majority of America's citizens."[1] For the purposes of state representation in Congress, Negro slaves counted as three-fifths of a person, under the original Constitution. For the purposes of voting, white women as well as male and female slaves were excluded. Since women's right to vote was not secured until the Nineteenth Amendment was ratified in 1920, women are recognizing not two centennials, but seven-tenths of a single century. Women need to ask themselves: In what way is this our bicentennial?

An answer to this question depends on how women choose to look upon the Constitution. They could regard the Constitution instrumentally — as providing them with particular rights, the right to vote, the right to equality. These particular rights might be deemed important much as an employee's contract with an employer guarantees a particular wage and benefit package. But there is another way to look upon the Constitution, and that is to see it as a document, ever-changing, around which there has been sustained and intense political struggle. Looked upon in this way, we are then called upon to judge the Constitution by what was learned in the struggle to change it.

Women, then, can celebrate the Constitution and their right to vote because their constitutional *struggles* to secure their rights have invested them with a broader sense of political possibilities. The political process — not merely the Constitutional product — invites our attention.

In this essay, I intend to explore the political consequences of victory and defeat, to look at how mobilization around the vote and around the modern Equal Rights Amendment (ERA) led women to pursue in their own very different and specific ways, their particular struggles for equality.

I present this argument in two parts — by looking at the aftermath of suffrage (the decade of the 1920s) and by analyzing the aftermath of the modern battle over the ERA (the decade of the 1980s).

My argument takes issue with a certain kind of scholarly and popular wisdom that describes the 1920s and 1980s in strikingly similar terms. Both decades are seen as periods when the women's movement collapsed. Recent feminist scholarship depicts the 1920s as a decade in which the women's movement, or at least gender-consciousness segments of it, disintegrated. This has a familiar ring: increasingly we hear such commentary about the 1980s — that the women's movement has run its course. The explanation of the movement-collapse phenomenon has an echo as well. We hear it argued that each movement concentrated its energies too narrowly on a single goal. Whether that goal was suffrage (and succeeded) or whether it was the ERA (and failed), it is claimed that the focus on a single goal made the women's movement vulnerable. If one subscribes to this line of reasoning, the lessons of the twenties and eighties might be that women put too much faith in the power of the vote or in the promise of constitutional change.

The 1920s.

I am going to argue against this movement-collapse thesis. The recent, substantial feminist scholarship on this period challenges earlier interpretations that assess the twenties in terms of the unkept "promises" of suffragist claims. This new scholarship, for instance, disputes the long-held view that suffrage failed to produce long-term political gains for women, because a women's voting bloc did not materialize. Feminist scholars note instead that although such a bloc did not materialize, women were not the passive voters that they have been depicted as being.[2] This new scholarship also challenges the old view that pronounced suffrage a failure for not delivering on the promise that the women's vote would clean up the cities and bring about moral, corruption-free governance. When asked whether women's suffrage was a failure, recent scholars cite the words of turn-of-the-century social reformer Jane Addams, who said, "Why don't you ask if suffrage in general is failing?" or militant suffragist Alice Paul, who queried, "Why not ask if this country is better off because men have voted for the last four years, the last forty years or a hundred years?"[3]

But in some ways, this recent scholarship still presents the 1920s as a period of decline and disintegration. After suffrage, most historians now argue, the feminist movement lost its cohesiveness, and gender consciousness waned.[4]

It should be understood, however, that the new generation of women in the twenties set out into a different world — one in which women could assume the rights for which their mothers and grandmothers struggled so hard. Certainly this new generation had different concerns. As historian Susan Ware notes, young college women of the 1920s spent their time ". . . smoking in public, bobbing their hair, discarding their corsets and even openly discussing sex . . . ," signs of loosening constraints on women's public behavior. Lillian Hellman, born in 1905, said that she grew up in a generation of women in the 1920s for whom women's emancipation was "stale stuff."[5]

But what about the older generation — the women born in the 1880s and 1890s — who were in their thirties and forties when suffrage was won? According to Yale historian Nancy Cott, this older generation would not have found in women's organizations of the 1920s the ". . . emphasis on womanhood — the proudly sex-defined sentiment that had powered so many earlier associations."[6]

The bottom line of the recent feminist scholarship is this: after the mid-1920s, there are few successes which can be claimed by feminist reformers. The Sheppard-Towner Acts (establishing maternal and child health care) and the Cable Acts (giving women married to foreigners their own rights of citizenship) were successes of the first half of the decade. The next half-decade saw little in the way of legislative victories. Gender consciousness, moreover, dissipated. According to Cott, women moved beyond the view that prevailed before suffrage — the view that women were different and that it was this difference that made their vote important. Instead, many women sought to promulgate a belief in gender-irrelevancy or gender-neutrality.

The story I see unfolding in the 1920s, in the aftermath of suffrage, is different. Perhaps it is a question of seeing the bottle as half full rather than half empty. I see this decade as a period in which women were enormously motivated by the struggles over suffrage, by the entitlement recognized through enfranchisement of their rightful place within the public sphere. The 1920s looks to me like a period of intense activism, aimed at achieving ever-increasing autonomy for women, broadening the spheres within which women can live their daily lives. This is not a period in which women call for a return to the home — to the obligations of mothering. It is a decade in which women's pursuits proliferate, their social and political commitments expand. It is a period not of narrowing in but of broadening out. It *is* the case that many women disavowed notions of women's different nature and women's special moral calling. This kind of gender consciousness was set aside. But many women continued to sense the need to break down barriers of discrimination and work collectively as women to establish claims to equality.

Indeed, the twenties saw an outbreak of new organizational activities by women — social reform organizations, professional associations, pacifist groups, and groups such as heterodoxy or the National Women's Party that explicitly took on the feminist label. With the achievement of suffrage, women's organizations mushroomed. Women's professional associations proliferated before, during, and after the suffrage movement reached its final phase during World War I. They included organizations of physicians, geographers, lawyers, bankers, journalists, women deans, dietitians, teachers, religious women, medical record librarians, dental hygienists, architects, public health nurses, dentists, medical technicians.[7]

The Women's Joint Congressional Committee, formed in 1920, worked together with the League of Women Voters, founded as the successor organization to the National American Women Suffrage Association. The National Women's Party proposed and championed an ERA; social reform organizations such as the National Consumer League worked for child labor restrictions, for the minimum wage laws and for protective labor legislation; the General Federation of Women's Clubs addressed themselves to the problems of medical services and educational facilities for Indians; groups of white women in the South resisted the ideology espousing the protection of white womanhood that had justified the practice of lynching and banded together in a "revolt against chivalry" to form anti-lynching campaigns.[8]

Together many of these organizations worked to gain women full citizenship: the right not only to vote but to serve in office; the right to serve on juries, the right to an American passport based on a woman's own nationality and not that of her husband's. And in the decade of the twenties, women entered nearly every aspect of government service. Only one woman held a major position in the federal government up to 1918; by 1929 nearly 200 women were appointed to administrative and supervisory posts. The Foreign Service was opened to women, new departments unlocked their doors, and the Bureau of Home Economics and the Women's Bureau were created, staffed, and run by women.[9]

It is true that women's groups were often divided on key issues, that some women disavowed a gender identity and sought instead to convince society of the irrelevance of gender. And as women developed in their professions, they sometimes sought professional advance at the expense of social reform concerns. But it is nevertheless the case that the struggle for suffrage did not lead to the abandonment of women's goals. Quite the reverse. After 1920 women's organizations worked to establish opportunities for women in walks of life as yet untried; they worked to secure for women the full entitlements of citizenship. Many worked for a more equitable society in which the burdens of race and poverty would be alleviated. These were women who were energized, not pacified by suffrage; they were motivated towards, not deterred from their new right to a place in the public forums of society.

The 1980s.

The 1980s tell a similar story. As with the 1920s, the argument so often heard nowadays is that the women's movement is in decline. We need to take a closer look. Although it is the case that public protest and demonstrations by women are less frequent than they were in the 1970s while the campaign for the ERA was under way, and although it is also true that protests by women today are limited largely to the issue of abortion, another kind of activism continues to be vibrant. Due in part to the struggle around the ERA, feminist consciousness has grown steadily from the 1970s onward. Propelled by the ideal of equal rights that the ERA campaign once again vocalized, feminist activists have mobilized unobtrusively inside the institutions of higher education, inside charitable foundations, the social services, the media, the professions, the church, and the armed forces — *inside the core institutions of American society and the American state.*

This unobtrusive mobilization is reflected in the dramatic and continued spread of feminist consciousness. A 1986 Gallup poll reports that at least one of every two white women and two of every three non-white women identify themselves as feminists. An even larger majority (71 percent) report their lives to have been improved by the feminist movement. Even women who explicitly reject feminism as a self-description have come to support core feminist ideas. Of the women who identify themselves as non-feminists in this same Gallup survey (the familiar "I'm not a feminist but . . ."), two-thirds support the idea of an ERA.[10]

This consciousness is generated inside numerous institutions, networks and associations. These organizations are diverse, dispersed through different sectors of the economy, society and politics. They are located in the voluntary sector (battered women's crisis groups), inside the professions (American Women in Radio and Television), in the union movement (Coalition for Labor Union Women), in the Congress (Congressional Caucus for Women's Issues), and in the churches (the Religious Network for Equality for Women).

I know of no way to get a numerical count of the decentralized, dispersed and unobtrusive organizing that operates outside the arena of national politics. But it is clear that these organizations are prolific. As I tell colleagues about my interest in women's organizations, I am consistently directed to look at this caucus or that organization: What about the Women's Caucus for Art? What about WISP, the organization of Women in Scholarly Publishing? Have I looked at women's computer networks? What about Sisters in Crime, started when a woman mystery writer drew attention to the fact that mystery writers of America had failed to award a woman the prize for best novel any time in the previous fifteen years? Had I known of Guerrilla Girls (women who dress in Guerrilla costumes, who make early morning assaults on New York's Metropolitan Museum, and who poster the walls of New York City's Soho district to protest the exclusion of women artists in important exhibitions)? What about Model Mugging — a woman's self-defense class? Or the Coal Mining Women's Support Team in Virginia, whose mimeographed newsletter in pastel pinks, greens, and blues alternates news of women who have fought discrimination and harassment in the mines with birthday wishes to one subscriber and condolences on a family illness to another? What about the just-recognized clerical union at Harvard University?

But the clearest influence of the ERA can be observed in the stirrings that began inside two of the core institutions of American society and the American state — the Catholic Church and the U.S. Armed Forces. The emergence of feminist activism in the Church can be traced to two influences: the inspiration of Vatican II's call for renewal (that brought women religious out of the more contemplative and strict practices of convent life into the community) and to the important influence of second wave feminism that was voiced by the struggles over the ERA in the 1970s.

The timing is revealing. Large-scale feminist activism in the Church began with the Women's Ordination Conference (WOC) held in Detroit in 1975. This conference was followed by subsequent gatherings organized by the Women's Ordination Conference and Women Church Convergence attended by thousands of lay and religious women. By the late 1970s, women's organizations had multiplied: the National Association of Women Religious (NAWR), the National Coalition of American Nuns (NCAN), Las Hermanas, The National Black Sisters Conference, Women's Alliance for Theology, Ethics and Ritual (WATER), and eventually the Woman-Church Convergence (an umbrella group of 28 separate organizations).

In addition to the issue of ordination, many feminist activists in the Church are involved in social justice work (running shelters, doing prison projects, organizing in the sanctuary movement, working against racism, homophobia, U.S. intervention in Central America).

Women activists in the Catholic Church often speak out boldly and publicly against Church teaching, Church practices and the Church hierarchy. Sister Theresa Kane, who as head of the Sisters of Mercy and the Leadership/Conference of Women Religious was considered more a moderate than an extremist on Church issues, was asked to offer a short greeting to Pope John Paul II during his 1979 visit to the United States. When Sister Theresa publicly urged the Pope to give women access to all ministries in the Church, a landmark event in feminist Church history had occurred. At the closing address of the Women's Ordination Conference in Cincinnati, Sister Theresa observed, "The core of courage is rage. For each of us I pray for a passionate holy rage; a just anger in the face of injustice not to be confused with hatred or hostility."[11] And yet Sister Theresa's words sound restrained next to the more pronounced anger of the National Coalition of American Nuns that accused Church officials of "fascism," some female religious leaders of "appeasement," and the bishops for their "obsession with issues of sexuality and the homophobia which results . . . (while remaining silent on patriarchal crimes such as incest and rape)."[12]

The strategic approach of feminist activists in the armed forces is at first glance the very inverse of their church counterparts. Mission-oriented, team players, working for change from within, following the chain of command are often-repeated phrases that apply to women in uniform, as well as men. But there are, nonetheless, important berths of feminist activism in the military. Although activists in the services would mostly disavow the feminist label, many women in the services are frustrated by, and work actively to change policies that limit employment opportunity for women and that perpetuate sexual harassment and gender stigmatizing.

Inside the services, these issues are pursued by women officers working in manpower, personnel, and equal opportunity positions. Outside the services, these issues are followed by such groups as the all-Civilian Defense Advisory Committee on Women in the Services (DACOWITS) and the Women's Equity Action League (WEAL) Project on Women in the Military. It was a DACOWITS tour of the Pacific and of European bases in the last two years that led, for instance, to important exposes of sexual harassment. Such groups have sustained pressure on the military to open up increasing numbers of positions from which women had earlier been barred.[13]

Conclusion

In this discussion of gender and constitutional change, I have implicitly recognized three analytical models. The first looks upon granting the right to vote primarily as an instrument by which the state asserts its control, manages the electorate, and promotes the state's interest. Within this model, the campaigns for both suffrage and the ERA are seen as diverting women from oppositional politics, as diverting women from a gender-conscious battle against the state to secure their political rights. The second model sees the vote and constitutional change as an instrument not of state control but of *citizen* representation. It sees voting and constitutional guarantees for equal rights as assuring particular possibilities — the right to express political interests by electing sympathetic legislators and by providing for particular laws.

This essay, however, argues for a third approach: it sees the vote and constitutional guarantees as important primarily for the mobilizational possibilities they confer. The great battles for the vote and for the ERA acted as beacons that guided women not just at the time that they were fighting for their rights, but also for a substantial period thereafter in their many, variously situated struggles for equality.

In the 1920s, women demonstrated what they had learned from the century-long struggle for suffrage: not only that they had a right to the vote, but no less important, that they had a right to act as public persons — to be active in the open spaces of political life as citizens working for change in all spheres of society and politics.

Women took this newly asserted right and translated it into organized protests against lynching, into social reform efforts to gain restrictions against child labor, assurances of a minimum wage for women, and protective guarantees for women workers. They also translated this suffrage claim into the campaign for the Equal Rights Amendment, into claims for equality in the legislatures, to their rights to serve on juries, and to their rights to American citizenship irrespective of marriage. Guided by the beacon of suffrage, they organized many different associations to assist women who sought advancement in their professions, or to win women appointments to government jobs. In many of these efforts, women faced continuous obstruction and discouragement. But they were efforts nonetheless galvanized by the inspiration of the claim to political citizenship that the battle for suffrage so clearly represented.

In the 1980s, the battle for the ERA became the torch that motivated many women working towards equality within the core institutions of both state and society. Although the defeat of the ERA is a sign to some movement watchers that the women's movement has become ineffective and moribund, my argument is otherwise. Beginning in the period of the mobilization around the ERA (in the mid-1970s), operating off the national stage outside the arena of conventional politics, feminists moved to establish a presence in both church and military and more broadly in constituent institutions of American sociopolitical life. Feminists have moved the struggle for constitutional change from the arena of public politics into the preserves of the once most sacred of male institutions.

What can the decades of the 1920s and 1980s tell us about the two great constitutional struggles which have engaged the women of this century? What did the struggles for the right to vote and for the constitutional establishment of equal rights achieve? It is useful to think of these struggles much as we would regard the march that Indian leader Mohandas Gandhi led to the sea in 1930 to protest the British salt tax, or the American civil rights' lunch counter sit-ins of the 1960s. Their value did not lie simply in whether the British ceased their tax on salt or whether blacks were allowed the right to sit alongside whites at public dining counters. Their value lay at least as importantly in the demonstration of a great principle, in the declaration of a people's claim to equality, and in the mobilization of political consciousness that has inspired political action in the decades that followed.

The struggles for the suffrage in the early decades of this century and the battle over the ERA of recent times should not discourage us about the distance that at times still separates political reality from constitutional rights. Instead, we can find inspiration in the many ways in which these struggles and battles for constitutional recognition have energized women in the everyday process of political empowerment.

NOTES

1. Justice Thurgood Marshall, "Remarks on the Bicentennial of the U.S. Constitution," *Signs* 13 (Autumn 1987): 10-17.

2. Sara Alpern and Dale Baum, "Female Ballots: The Impact of the Nineteenth Amendment," *Journal of Interdisciplinary History* 16 (Summer 1985): 43-69.

3. J. Stanley Lemons, *The Woman Citizen: Social Feminism in the 1920s* (Urbana, Ill., 1973), 234.

4. See Nancy F. Cott, *The Grounding of Modern Feminism* (New Haven, Ct., 1987).

5. Susan Ware, *Beyond Suffrage: Women in the New Deal* (Cambridge, Mass., 1981), 20.

6. Cott, *Grounding,* 96.

7. Lemons, *The Woman Citizen,* 43.

8. Jacqueline Dawd Hall, *Revolt Against Chivalry: Jessie Daniel Ames and the Women's Campaign Against Lynching* (New York, 1979).

9. Lemons, *The Woman Citizen,* 80.

10. "Gallup Poll 1986," *Newsweek* 52 (March 31, 1986): 51.

11. *Commonweal* 114 (November 6, 1987): 613.

12. *National Catholic Register* 62 (December 14, 1986): 2.

13. Judith Hicks Stiehm, *Arms and the Enlisted Woman* (Philadelphia, 1979).

SUGGESTED READINGS

Chafe, William. *The American Woman: Her Changing Social, Economic, and Political Roles, 1920-1970.* New York: Oxford University Press, 1972.

Cott, Nancy F. *The Grounding of Modern Feminism.* New Haven: Yale University Press, 1987.

Flexner, Eleanor. *Century of Struggle: The Women's Rights Movement in the United States.* Revised. Cambridge, Mass.: Belknap Press of Harvard University Press, 1975.

Freedman, Estelle, "The New Woman: Changing Views of Women in the 1920s," in Lois Scharf and Joan M. Jensen, eds. *Decades of Discontent, The Women's Movement, 1920-1940.* Boston: Northeastern University Press, 1987, 21-42.

Hall, Jacquelyn Dowd. *Revolt Against Chivalry: Jessie Daniel Ames and the Women's Campaign Against Lynching.* New York: Columbia University Press, 1979.

Lemons, J. Stanley. *The Woman Citizen: Social Feminism in the 1920s.* Urbana: University of Illinois Press, 1973.

Stiehm, Judith Hicks. *Arms and the Enlisted Woman.* Philadelphia: Temple University Press, 1989.

Ware, Susan. *Beyond Suffrage: Women in the New Deal.* Cambridge, Mass.: Harvard University Press, 1981.

HANDS THAT PICKED COTTON...
NOW CAN PICK OUR PUBLIC OFFICIALS

VOTER EDUCATION PROJECT, INC., 52 FAIRLIE STREET, NW, ATLANTA, GEORGIA 30303 (404) 522-7495

REGISTER AND VOTE!

Poster from the Atlanta Voter Education Project, circa 1970, advocating black voter registration. Registering black voters, especially in the South, was one of the central aims of the modern Civil Rights Movement, since blacks had been politically inactive during the first half of the twentieth century, due to discriminatory southern laws and customs. *Source: Museum of American History, Smithsonian Institution.*

7 THE CONSTITUTION AND THE CIVIL RIGHTS MOVEMENT: THE QUEST FOR A MORE PERFECT UNION

Linda Faye Williams
Joint Center for Political Studies
Washington, D.C.

Although the Fifteenth Amendment forbade states from denying the right to vote on the basis of race, southern blacks were largely excluded from the political system during the first half of the twentieth century. During the two decades following the Civil War, blacks — most of them ex-slaves and nearly all of them still living in the South — actively participated in state and local politics, voting regularly and electing many black officials to office. In the 1890s, however, southern white Democrats systematically removed blacks from electoral politics through voting regulations such as the "grandfather clause" and literacy tests, through electoral procedures such as the all-white primary, and through physical intimidation. As a result, blacks were all but absent from southern politics until the Civil Rights Movement of the 1950s and 1960s.

Securing black voting rights in the South was one of the principal goals of the Movement. Through mass protests, voter registration drives, congressional lobbying and suits in federal courts, civil rights activists eliminated discriminatory southern electoral practices which kept blacks from the polls, and they secured federal protection of black political rights. The crowning achievement of this campaign was the Voting Rights Act of 1965, which outlawed unfair electoral procedures and required the Justice Department to supervise southern elections.

As Linda Faye Williams explains in the following essay, the Voting Rights Act was not only a central accomplishment of the Civil Rights Movement, but also a milestone in blacks' struggle for political representation. The act, she argues, has gone a long way toward reducing the gap between white and minority electoral participation, and it has improved black representation in the political arena.

This accomplishment, however, has led to other problems. While the Voting Rights Act has done much to re-enfranchise blacks, Williams contends, other electoral practices still stand in the way of a "meaningful ballot." Procedures such as at-large elections and multi-member districts deprive blacks of real political influence. The legacy of the Civil Rights Movement, then, is a mixed one, but the accomplishments made so far leave Williams optimistic for the future.

Neither the original Constitution, nor the Constitution as amended, is but a stupendous sham, keeping the promise to the eye and breaking it to the heart; they have promised us law and given us anarchy.

Frederick Douglass, 1886

The Constitution is a dirty rag, a cheat, a libel, and ought to be spit upon by every Negro in the land.

Henry McNeil Turner, 1886

Even one hundred years after the adoption of the United States Constitution and more than twenty years after a Civil War "to free the slaves," most black Americans remained deprived of the right to vote. Perhaps that one injustice, more than any other, accounted for the negative evaluations of the Constitution provided by Frederick Douglass and Henry McNeil Turner near the turn of the century.

When the nation celebrated the bicentennial of the Constitution in 1989, however, the disenfranchisement of blacks had been significantly altered. Despite the continuation of many barriers, by and large blacks can now vote.

This change is largely a result of the Civil Rights Movement of the 1950s and 1960s, the concomitant Voting Rights Act of 1965, and its reauthorization in 1982. The following discussion first establishes that blacks have made substantial progress in exercising their voting rights since 1965 and shows that one result of black voting has been the election of a historic number of black officials; second, it summarizes the remaining major impediments to effective black voting rights; and third, it projects some trends in black voting rights in the immediate future.

Black Voter Participation

The experience of blacks in seeking access to the electoral process has been unique. The Fourteenth and Fifteenth Amendments to the Constitution presumably bestowed full civil and political rights on blacks a century ago. Yet, for a majority of blacks, access to the electoral process has been won only after nearly a hundred years of struggle in the courts, in Congress, and through mass protests. Comparing the experience of blacks with that of other ethnic groups, political scientist Charles Hamilton noted that blacks have

had to devote a substantial amount of time and energy simply to establishing their claim to political citizenship. While the earlier ethnic groups could launch careers as precinct captains and political bargainers, blacks had to spend time as plaintiffs and protesters.[1]

Blacks faced special barriers imposed by numerous state and local laws and regulations, party rules, and unofficial but effective violence by whites. Their efforts to overcome these barriers and to eliminate other inequities in participation have profoundly altered the electoral process and ensured more equitable participation by other historically disadvantaged groups as well.

Indeed, the best available data demonstrate that blacks have made considerable progress relative to whites in political mobilization. In the first presidential election after passage of the Voting Rights Act (1968), the gap between black and white voter registration rates was 9.2 percentage points, and the gap between black and white voter turnout rates was 11.5 percentage points, according to the U.S. Census Bureau. By 1988, the black/white voter registration rate gap had fallen to 3.4 percentage points, and the black/white voter turnout gap was 7.6 percentage points. All in all, 51.5 percent of blacks and 59.1 percent of whites reported voting in 1988.

The trend has been the same in midterm congressional elections: the gap in voter turnout fell from 15.3 percentage points in 1966 to 3.8 percentage points in 1986. In a nation where voting patterns change slowly and in a period when the trend in turnout has been mostly downward, this narrowing of the voting gap between the races is strong evidence of disappearing barriers to voting by minorities.

Another indicator of electoral progress is rapid growth in the number of blacks elected to public office over the past two decades. The number grew from fewer than 500 in 1965 to 7,225 in 1989. The South, where most blacks remained disenfranchised until 1965, has been the region of greatest progress. In January 1989, there were sixty-two times more black elected officials in the South than there were in 1965 (4,854 compared to 78, respectively). Since approximately two out of every three black elected officials represents a majority black jurisdiction, the increase in the number of black elected officials is an important measure of black voting strength.[2]

Still another arena of progress has been in party politics. Historically, the two major parties reflected and accommodated the prejudices of the larger society and erected their own barriers to participation by minorities. In the South, for example, some blacks managed to obtain the franchise, but the long dominant Democratic party used mechanisms like the "white primary" to exclude them from the only meaningful exercise of the vote — the primary election. Furthermore, candidate-slating arrangements were adopted that virtually eliminated minorities' chances of winning nomination for public office.

Elimination of barriers to minority participation in the political parties has occurred slowly. The Republican party still remains basically a white people's bastion, but the adoption in the mid-1960s of proportionality principles requiring state party organizations to ensure the selection of delegations that reflected as nearly as possible the racial and gender composition of the party's electorate visibly has increased the influence of blacks in the Democratic party. Between 1964, when the last convention under the old order took place, and 1988, the proportion of black delegates to the Democratic party's national convention grew from 2.8 percent to 23.1 percent.[3] Perhaps, the best evidence of black access to influence in the Democratic party is the fact that Ronald Brown, a black man, is now the chair of the Democratic National Committee. More recently, for the first time, another black, Representative William Gray of Pennsylvania, has become the majority whip in the United States House of Representatives.

Today, then, blacks are not systematically denied the right to vote anywhere in the United States. Informal obstacles such as intimidation and bureaucratic obstructions continue to discourage voting in some localities, but continued voting rights activism and the growing power of the black electorate are likely to ensure gradual eradication of most remaining barriers.

Remaining Barriers

The considerable progress made by blacks in eliminating barriers to their electoral participation, however, has not occurred evenly across all parts of the process, and substantial barriers remain. These barriers include: 1) minority vote dilution through sophisticated legal and administrative barriers such as at-large electoral systems, racial gerrymandering, unfair candidate slating procedures, and runoff requirements; 2) class barriers to participation such as poverty and lack of education; 3) psychological barriers such as the lack of a habit of voting derived from years of exclusion from voting, fear, deference to whites, and apathy; and 4) institutional obstacles such as the problem of inadequate information concerning voter registration and procedures, the often inconvenient time and place of registration, and the scarcity of black registration officials, especially in the South.

This latter factor, burdensome registration requirements, is perhaps the principal impediment to black voting. The rules governing registration and voting vary from state to state (and in some states, such as Alabama, from county to county), but in most places there is one commonality: registration rules are not designed to simplify participation. On the contrary, registration requirements are typically burdensome enough to discourage voting by all but the highly motivated. According to several social scientists, registration laws make voting more difficult in the United States than in almost any other western democracy. The resulting reduction in turnout has been estimated to be anywhere from 9 to 15 percent. Complex voter registration requirements have the greatest vote-inhibiting effect, according to these social scientists, among lower socioeconomic groups, within which minorities are disproportionately represented.[4]

Thus, even after the removal of blatantly discriminatory registration procedures, blacks and other low-income voters continue to face hardships in registering to vote. Especially in southern localities, individuals must travel miles to the county seat to register at offices that are open only on weekdays during working hours. In addition, some of these localities purge the voter rolls frequently, making it necessary for many citizens to reregister at relatively frequent intervals. Partly because of these continuing obstacles, considerable private resources have been spent on costly, labor-intensive campaigns to get otherwise eligible minorities registered to vote.

Many voting rights advocates now seek to achieve "equal ballot access" for blacks by making registration much easier. Some are using lawsuits to challenge registration arrangements that primarily obstruct minorities in the South. Others are lobbying state and local officials to institute registration by mail, registration in government agencies extensively used by the poor, or registration on the same day of voting. Currently, Congress is considering legislation which would mandate simplified registration procedures for all federal elections.

Other barriers reduce the impact of black voting. At-large or multi-member districts and racial gerrymanders are still widely used to effectively stack the electoral system against blacks and other minorities. Vote dilution through racial gerrymandering and multi-member districts has been ruled unconstitutional by the U.S. Supreme Court. In 1960, the Court outlawed the racial gerrymander in *Gomillion* v. *Lightfoot.* Thirteen years later, in *White* v. *Regester,* it held that an at-large electoral arrangement was unconstitutional on the ground that it diluted black and Hispanic votes.

The remaining problem, however, is establishing the evidentiary standard to be employed in determining when a multi-member district is unconstitutional. In *Mobile* v. *Bolden* (1980), the Court overturned a lower court finding that the at-large election system of Mobile, Alabama, unconstitutionally diluted black votes, and ruled that the plaintiffs had not established the city's intent to discriminate. This "intent" test, as opposed to an "effect" test used by the lower courts, posed an almost insurmountable obstacle to further legal challenges to vote-diluting electoral arrangements. The Court's decision prompted considerable attention to the evidentiary issue and resulted in an amendment to section two of the Voting Rights Act by Congress in 1982, undoing the Supreme Court's *Mobile* ruling by instituting the effects or results test.

In *Thornburg* v. *Gingles* (1986), the Supreme Court had its first clear opportunity to revisit the vote-dilution issue using the new standard established by the Voting Rights Act amendments. At issue was a challenge to a system composed of six multi-member districts and one single-member district in North Carolina that, blacks alleged, deprived them of a fair opportunity to elect a candidate of their choice. In upholding the lower court's decision outlawing these electoral arrangements, the Supreme Court used the effects test to pave the way for challenges in similar electoral arrangements throughout the country.

The shift in emphasis from combating traditional forms of vote denial to vote dilution has at least two important implications. First, it raises new and more complex issues with respect to representation and consequently imposes new evidentiary demands. What blacks and other minorities are now seeking is not merely the right to cast a ballot, but the right to cast a "meaningful" ballot. The courts have accepted the argument that the dilution of a group's voting strength through structural electoral arrangements is unconstitutional whether intended or not. The evidence required for a showing of dilution is primarily the minority group's experience in electing its members to legislative bodies in the context of a history of racially polarized voting. However, both the criteria and the concept of bloc voting remain controversial.

Second, the focus on the right to a meaningful ballot expands the challenge beyond state and local legislative elections in the South. In one of the first vote-dilution challenges outside the South, the Federal District Court for Central Illinois found that the city of Springfield's commission form of government, with its at-large election system and history of racially polarized voting, denied blacks a reasonable opportunity to elect candidates of their choice. The court ordered the city to replace the at-large commission with a council elected by wards. Several other cities outside of the South with similar government structures and voting histories have been successfully challenged by the courts.

In short, blacks' and other minorities' continuing challenge to election structures and procedures has prompted the courts to consider anew what constitutes equal participation and how it is achieved. Although definitive answers are not yet available, understanding of the electoral process and the status of minorities in it is being considerably enhanced by the search.

Toward the Immediate Political Future

The experience since the mid-1960s provides grounds for optimism about the prospects for increasing minority access to the electoral process. That experience underscores both the flexibility of the constitutional system and the efficacy of Civil Rights protest strategies, enhanced minority voting, and continued court litigation for inducing electoral change.

Yet, the system has also demonstrated the capacity to resist demands for reform. Many of the recent gains are relatively tenuous and slight. For example, despite the growth in the number of black elected officials, it is wise to note that these black officials still compose only 1.4 percent of the total number of elected officials in the nation, while blacks compose 11.2 percent of the voting age population. Similarly, there is only one black governor (Virginia), and there are no black U.S. senators in the nation. Moreover, even the gains made could be undone by the altered judicial climate in the nation today or even changes in the electoral strategies of the two major political parties.

In the two decades since the late 1960s, the pattern of institutional support for civil rights has changed a good deal. The U.S. Supreme Court under Chief Justices Warren Burger and William Rehnquist has been a less reliable supporter of civil rights claims than was the Court under Chief Justice Earl Warren. Moreover, during Ronald Reagan's term in office, 1981-1989, the presidency came to be seen as anything but a bully pulpit for equal voting rights. Instead, Reagan first opposed reauthorization of the Voting Rights Act of 1982. Civil rights activists argue that only the probability that Congress would override his veto transformed President Reagan from an opponent into a "supporter." Many observers add, moreover, that having reluctantly supported the Voting Rights Act reauthorization, Reagan then weakened its force through under-enforcement by the Justice Department.

More debilitating in the long run was the Reagan administration's attack on activist federal courts that often ruled in favor of civil rights in the 1960s. Reagan's appointments to the lower federal bench are already implementing the Reagan conservative agenda. Several analyses of federal district court decisions from 1981 to 1985 revealed judges appointed by President Jimmy Carter were more likely to support the voting rights of disadvantaged minorities than Reagan appointees. The massive campaign against the nomination of Appeals Court Judge Robert Bork to the U.S. Supreme Court reflected an awareness that Reagan's nominees were moving the Court away from its earlier commitment to equal voting and other civil rights.

Still another factor that could sustain barriers to minority participation, paradoxically, is party competition. Arguably, race has been the most powerful single issue in American politics. The two major parties and several of the minor ones often defined themselves or were defined in relation to that issue. Thus, for nearly a century after the Civil War, the Republican party's platform was to some extent defined by its position on emancipation, reconstruction, and basic civil rights for blacks. During this time the Republicans functioned almost exclusively in the North, while the Democratic party endeared itself to southern whites by espousing white supremacy. During the New Deal of the 1930s, a shift in partisanship occurred among many groups (including blacks) as a result of social welfare policies rather than race-related issues. By 1948, however, strains in the New Deal party system had already begun to occur. Ever since Senator Strom Thurmond led white southerners out of the Democratic party's convention and formed the Dixiecrat party in 1948, white southerners have left the Democratic party in droves.

Meanwhile, as the Democrats came more and more to embrace civil rights for blacks, blacks to the tune of 94 percent of black voters in 1984 have supported the Democratic party. The last time a majority of white southerners supported the Democratic party's nominee for president and the last time more than 20 percent of blacks supported the Republican party's nominee was in 1964.

These racial patterns in partisan support have influenced minorities' struggle for greater access to political power in general and for greater influence over party affairs in particular. For example, behind the push by Presidents John F. Kennedy and Lyndon B. Johnson to expand black voting rights in the 1960s was the need to shore up the Democratic party's support in the South. Undoubtedly, expanding black voting rights will continue to be influenced by the competitive needs of the parties in the electorate. Already, there are signs that the Democratic party is becoming increasingly uncomfortable about its strong identification with blacks and might be seeking to reduce that identification as it tries to woo southern white voters again. Such efforts may become especially blatant in the battle over redistricting after the 1990s reapportionment of Congressional districts.

On the other hand, the Republican party does not appear likely to regain control of the House of Representatives and perhaps even the U.S. Senate in the next few elections, unless it can split off at least a substantial minority of the black vote. Toward that end, Republican party chairman Lee Atwater has announced a plan to go after the black vote. If the Republicans can win just 20 percent of the black vote in many congressional districts and several states, this small proportion alone would be enough to neutralize the impact of blacks in favor of the Democrats. Just how these partisan efforts play out will go a long way toward determining whether black influence in Democratic party politics and American elections continues to expand or recede.

Finally, although the gains made through the courts and through pressure on the political parties greatly facilitate fuller and effective minority political participation, that goal cannot be realized until white voters are willing to accept minorities as legitimate, competent participants in all phases of the political process, especially as candidates for elective office.

Progress in this regard has been grudgingly slow. Generally, no more than 20 percent of whites have demonstrated a willingness to vote for black candidates for local offices such as mayor. To be sure, several 1989 mayoral races demonstrated exceptions to this problem. David Dinkins of New York City, Norman Rice of Seattle, John Daniels of New Haven, and Mark White of Cleveland all won more than 35 percent of the white vote. Their victories were widely publicized, however, precisely because they were exceptions to the rule. Jesse Jackson's experience illustrates the norm. Although he made substantial progress in winning the votes of whites in his two races for president in 1984 and 1988, Jackson still won only about the usual proportion of a highly popular black candidate for office (17 percent of white Democratic primary voters in 1988 compared to 5 percent in 1984).

The scarce data on white attitudes toward black candidates for public office suggest that racial attitudes remain a formidable barrier to black electoral success. In 1988, when the Joint Center for Political Studies Gallup survey asked whites whether they would vote for a generally well-qualified man for president "if he happened to be black," 77 percent said they would. However, when asked if there is a "qualified" black on the current American political scene, only 21 percent reported that there is a black qualified to be president. This means that almost eight out of every ten whites would require a lot of convincing even to consider a black candidate qualified to be president. Moreover, the same survey found that 56 percent of white respondents reported that whites are more likely to vote on the basis of race rather than qualifications when a black candidate was opposed by a white one. In an electoral arena as intensely competitive as the American one, these attitudes constitute truly formidable obstacles to blacks. The removal of structural and procedural barriers to participation will improve the level of minority participation in the electoral process, but change in white attitudes also is essential.

Conclusion

The problem of unequal voting rights has flawed American politics and promoted a vigorous struggle to achieve a more open, democratic system. This struggle was at no time more evident or more successful than in the Civil Rights Movement of the 1950s and 1960s. The struggle engendered in the Movement has influenced the electoral process in at least two important ways. First, it has helped bring into being a fuller universal adult suffrage by eradicating or reducing obstacles to the poor as well as to minorities. Second, it has expanded the concept of equality in the electoral arena to include not only the right to vote but the right to cast a meaningful ballot.

These developments will by no means ensure the democratic ideal of an equal voice for each individual. Nor is it at all clear that voting rights will produce many tangible benefits in the socioeconomic sphere. Some cities with black mayors for fifteen years or more, for example, have larger numbers and proportions of blacks in poverty today than they had before blacks gained access to political power. Money has been and will continue to be the single most powerful force in the electoral and socioeconomic arenas. As long as there are major disparities in wealth and income between minorities and the white majority, money is likely to stack even the electoral system against minorities. Similarly, disparities in education and the long tradition of political nonparticipation will continue to disadvantage minorities.

Yet, as Americans celebrate the two hundredth anniversary of the Constitution, there is substantial evidence in the nation's electoral politics that even Frederick Douglass and Henry McNeil Turner, if alive today, would surely agree: important strides have been made in fulfilling the quest for a more perfect union.

NOTES

1. Charles V. Hamilton, "Political Access, Minority Participation, and the New Normalcy," in Leslie W. Dunbar, ed., *Minority Report: What Has Happened to Blacks, Hispanics, American Indians, and Other Minorities in the Eighties* (New York, 1984), 11.

2. Data on black elected officials from Joint Center for Political Studies, *Black Elected Officials: A National Roster 1989* (Washington, D.C., 1989).

3. Joint Center for Political Studies, *Blacks and the 1988 Democratic Convention* (Washington, D.C., 1988).

4. For a discussion of the impact of registration laws on voter turnout, see G. Bingham Powell, Jr., "American Voter Turnout in Comparative Perspective," *American Political Science Review* 80 (March 1986): 20-36; Steven J. Rosenstone and Raymond Wolfinger, "The Effect of Registration Laws on Voter Turnout," *American Political Science Review* 72 (March 1978): 22-45; and Jack Bass, "Election Laws and their Manipulation to Exclude Minority Voters," in *The Right to Vote: A Rockefeller Foundation Conference* (New York, 1981), 1-32.

SUGGESTED READINGS

Bass, Jack. "Election Laws and their Manipulation to Exclude Minority Voters." In *The Right to Vote: A Rockefeller Foundation Conference,* 1-32. New York: Rockefeller Foundation, 1981.

Daniels, William J. "The Constitution, the Supreme Court, and Racism: Compromises on the Way to Democracy," *National Political Science Review* 1 (1989): 126-133.

Davidson, Chandler, ed. *Minority Vote Dilution.* Washington, D.C.: Howard University Press, 1984.

Foster, Lorn S., ed. *The Voting Rights Act: Consequences and Implications.* New York: Praeger, 1985.

Hamilton, Charles V. "Political Access, Minority Participation, and the New Normalcy." In *Minority Report: What Has Happened to Blacks, Hispanics, American Indians, and Other Minorities in the Eighties,* edited by Leslie W. Dunbar, 11. New York: Pantheon Books, 1984.

Joint Center for Political Studies. *Black Elected Officials: A National Roster 1989.* Washington, D.C.: JCPS Press, 1989.

Joint Center for Political Studies. *Blacks and the 1988 Democratic Convention.* Washington, D.C.: JCPS Press, 1988.

Morris, Aldon. *The Origins of the Civil Rights Movement: Black Communities Organizing for Change.* New York: The Free Press, 1984.

Piven, Frances Fox and Richard Cloward. *Poor Peoples Movements: How They Succeed, Why Some Fail.* New York: Vintage Books, 1979.

Powell, G. Bingham, Jr. "American Voter Turnout in Comparative Perspective." *American Political Science Review* 80 (March 1986): 20-36.

Rosenstone, Steven J. and Raymond Wolfinger. "The Effect of Registration Laws on Voter Turnout." *American Political Science Review* 72 (March 1978): 22-45.

Scheingold, Stuart A. *The Politics of Rights: Lawyers, Public Policy, and Political Change.* New Haven: Yale University Press, 1974.

Selected "get out the vote" material from the 1950s and 1960s. Low voter turnout and growing voter apathy have been major problems in American politics since the 1920s. *Source: Museum of American Political Life, University of Hartford.*

8 PARTICIPATION IN AMERICAN ELECTIONS†

Everett Carll Ladd
Roper Center for Public Opinion Research
University of Connecticut

Americans pride themselves for having what they regard as the most advanced democracy in the world. The Bill of Rights guarantees regarding freedom of expression, freedom of the press, and freedom of religion, the openness of the American political party system, the frequency of elections at every level of government, and most important, the broad extension of the right to vote to virtually all adult citizens make the United States one of the most representative and open political systems in the world.

Nonetheless, recent voting trends have caused many Americans to worry. Despite the broad extension of suffrage rights, the proportion of Americans who actually go to the polls and exercise their franchise in national elections has gradually declined in the twentieth century. Compared to statistics from other democracies, the rate of voter turnout in the United States is alarmingly low.

Declining American voter turnout has led many commentators to speculate that American democracy itself may be in decline. Some observers suggest that so many people — particularly minorities and the poor — do not vote that American government is no longer representative of all of the people. Others contend that low voter turnout is a reflection of a flagging commitment of Americans to their civic duties — as part of the most successful and prosperous democracy in history, many citizens have become too comfortable and apathetic.

In the essay that follows, Everett Carll Ladd challenges these popular reactions to contemporary American voter turnout. While admitting that turnout has been declining, Ladd contends that the variation between voter behavior in the United States and in other democracies is partly a statistical illusion generated by different methods of measurement. More importantly, he also argues that the significance of voter turnout cannot be truly appreciated without closely examining the institutional and social factors that influence it. Contrary to the prevailing popular view that American democracy is "in trouble," Ladd maintains that political participation, if not turnout in national elections, remains very high, leading him to conclude that democracy in America is still lively and vibrant.

†Reprinted from Everett Carll Ladd, *The American Polity: The People and Their Government* (New York: W.W. Norton & Company, 1989), 416-426.

As the franchise has been guaranteed to all citizens through Constitutional amendments, legislative, executive, and judicial action, and political development, there has been a heightening of concern over the relatively low proportion of eligible voters who actually cast ballots. According to official statistics, only 53 percent of voting-age residents voted in the 1984 presidential election, 10 percent below the turnout in the 1960 Kennedy-Nixon contest. An even smaller proportion — roughly 51 percent of the voting-age population — participated in the 1988 presidential contest.

Turnout is even lower in voting for the U.S. House of Representatives. In 1976 it dropped below the 50 percent mark for the first time in a presidential election year since the 1940s, and it was only 48 percent in 1984. In "off-year" voting for the House, without the added spur and visibility of the more publicized presidential contest, participation is lower still. Only 38 percent of the voting-age public participated in the 1982 House contests, and just 38 percent voted in 1986.

A Confounding Decline

Our country's low and somewhat declining voter participation is made more striking by its occurrence in the face of developments designed to spur voting. The drop-off in turnout of the last decade and a half has taken place at the very time the poll tax was outlawed, discrimination at polling places on the basis of race or language was prohibited, residency requirements were greatly eased, unreasonable registration dates were discarded, and many states initiated procedures to enhance participation such as mobile registrars, postcard registration, and every election-day registration.[1] Other developments associated with higher participation have also been occurring, the most notable of which is the steady increase in the extent of formal education. As data presented later in this essay show, the strongest observed link between social characteristics of the population and inclination to vote involves education: the more of it citizens have, the higher their participation levels in elections of all types.[2] And yet as the formal education of the populace has been growing so impressively, voter turnout has been falling.

Concern has been spurred further by comparisons of voter turnout in the United States to that in other democracies. Although, as we will see, comparisons are more difficult to make than is sometimes supposed, the mean (or average) turnout in national elections from 1945 to 1980 was 95 percent in Australia and the Netherlands, 87 percent in West Germany, 81 percent in Norway, 79 percent in France, 77 percent in Great Britain, 76 percent in Canada, and 73 percent in Japan — while in American presidential elections during this period turnout was just 59 percent.

Is Voter Turnout a Problem?

The United States is the world's oldest democracy and a pioneer in the extension of the vote to the entire population, but it appears to have one of the lowest voter-participation rates among the world's democracies. The U.S. has taken a number of measures to spur registration and the population now seems better equipped to vote, given its high formal education, but still turnout is falling off. A debate is going on over the source and nature of the problem and its consequences.

Some argue that low turnout diminishes the capacity of those not participating to represent their interests and shape policy. For example, after reviewing data suggesting that the decline in turnout between 1960 and 1976 did not take place evenly across the population but was sharpest among whites of low income and education, Howard Reiter expressed concern that this "may make federal policy-makers less responsive to their [lower-status whites'] desires than they used to be. This may be especially significant for the Democratic party, which has claimed to speak for lower and working-class interests."[3] Frances Fox Piven and Richard Cloward maintain that U.S. voter registration statutes requiring that individuals themselves come forward to get registered — rather than being registered automatically by a government agency — are in fact a greater barrier to the poor than to the affluent. As a result, these statutes serve to underrepresent the poor and shift the electorate more to the political right than it otherwise would be.[4]

Other experts disagree. Ruy A. Teixeira argues that "quite simply, for many Americans, voting just doesn't seem worth the bother. . . . Nonvoting [is hardly] an indicator of suppressed radicalism or any other political viewpoint." While nonvoters differ from voters in some regards, such as educational background, they don't differ much in political outlook. From a partisan point of view, "the question of mobilizing nonvoters is logically inseparable from the question of mobilizing voters. A party unable to sway the existing pool of voters with its message would be unlikely to change its fortunes by mobilizing more nonvoters to vote."[5]

Voter participation is central to the democratic process, and the debate over the consequences of nonvoting is an important one. As we will see, however, the whole subject of who votes and who doesn't and what this means is quite complicated. We need to try to assemble some pertinent information. One source of confusion on American voter turnout as opposed to other democracies is the lack of fully comparable statistics. The conclusion that we have already drawn from our data — that voter turnout is lower here than abroad — is valid. But important qualifications on this conclusion are often overlooked. Voter turnout for the United States is regularly computed on the basis of votes as a percentage of the *voting-age population;* in all other countries, turnout is calculated on votes cast as a percentage of *registered voters.* Additionally, in the United States only valid votes are counted in the total turnout, while in the other countries invalid and blank ballots are also in the total figure. These statistical dissimilarities make turnout in the United States seem lower than it actually is.

Part of the reason why data are published with one statistical convention for the United States and another elsewhere is that American registration laws result in a substantial proportion of the voting-age population not being registered in any given election. Most other democracies, however, have registration procedures intended to register virtually the entire adult citizenry automatically; for these nations measuring turnout as a proportion of registered voters is appropriate. But as British political scientist Ivor Crewe has pointed out, "The accuracy of the turnout figures [for all countries except the United States] depends on the efficiency of the electoral registers on which they are all based. . . ."[6] In those instances where "the registers omit those unlikely to exercise their right to vote (the homeless, tenants of single rooms, immigrants), *turnout figures will be artificially inflated.*" Any situation where significant numbers of people are not counted among registered voters makes turnout appear higher than it really is; computing turnout on the basis of those registered always inflates participation rates since no registration system ever records all voting-age residents.

At the time of the 1984 U.S. presidential election, the noninstitutionalized voting-age population of the United States was about 172 million. The number of valid ballots cast for president was 92.7 million — hence the turnout figure of just over 53 percent. But just 115 million Americans were registered to vote in 1984. Among those who were registered, the turnout was 80 percent. (See Table 1, page 117.)

Why were fifty-seven million voting-age residents of the United States not registered? Certainly many of them did not register, because they did not intend to vote. Registration and voting in the United States are part of one continuous act of electoral participation. The government does not assume the responsibility of registering people but rather requires that citizens initiate the step; millions of people who for whatever reason do not plan to vote, just do not register. But among the unregistered residents are millions who are off the rolls not because of lack of interest, but because by law they cannot register or vote. Perhaps as many as nine million resident aliens of voting age in the United States don't have the citizenship required for voting. The Census figures on voting-age residents also regularly include "institutional" populations. Those jailed for felonies are barred by law from registering and voting. Many other people who are institutionalized, like inmates of mental facilities, cannot vote. All of this means that millions of people in the United States who are of voting age are barred from registration by reasonable, consciously developed legal standards. By continuing to compute turnout on the basis of all those of voting age, we substantially overstate the magnitude of American nonvoting.

Voter Participation across History

If turnout is low in America, it has long been that way. Participation in the presidential election of 1924 (as a percentage of the voting-age population) was just 43 percent, 8 percentage points lower than in 1988. And electoral participation in 1936 was only slightly higher than at present. There is a large dimension to nonvoting in the United States unrelated to dissatisfaction with democratic performance or with the parties and their leaders. As Seymour M. Lipset, among others, has noted, American nonvoting is "a reflection of the stability of the system" and confidence that the next election will not produce threatening or dangerous results.[7] Elections in many countries involve contenders far more dissimilar in their programs and outlooks than are the Democrats and Republicans in the United States. The two major American political parties are middle-class alliances that share many basic ideological commitments. For a Democrat, the prospect of a Republican being elected is not usually wildly threatening, and vice versa. Less interested or involved people are more likely to participate electorally in contests where they see the stakes to be high. As a stable democracy that has operated under the same constitutional structure for two centuries, the United States has a political system that is not so stress-filled, and many people feel they can afford the luxury of not voting.

One rebuttal to this argument is that voter turnout was much higher in the United States in the late-nineteenth century than at present. According to data collected by Walter Dean Burnham, voter turnout was 75 percent in the presidential election of 1892, 79 percent in 1896 and 73 percent in 1900.[8] Turnout undoubtedly was higher in the last century than in our own, but not as much higher as these statistics would suggest. Voting fraud occurred more frequently in the nineteenth century because it could be committed so easily.

Stipulations on eligibility requirements were few and easily avoided. The paper ballots were printed by the political parties, not by the government. The counting of votes was often controlled by the parties and, in areas of one-party dominance, padding of the totals was commonplace. As a result, the number of votes reported in nineteenth-century elections was probably, as a routine matter, considerably larger than the number of voting-age citizens actually casting ballots. One often-cited instance of exaggeration of turnout is that of West Virginia, where the reported turnout in 1888 was actually twelve thousand votes higher than the total of those eligible to vote!

Sources of Diminished Voter Turnout

When all these factors are considered, it is still clear that current voter turnout in the United States has dropped off over the last quarter-century. One reason involves the status of political parties, which have undergone in recent decades a great variety of changes. While it is certainly not true that all of these shifts have left them weaker than they were in earlier eras, *local party organizations* have on the whole been weakened. In times past, strong local party organizations had the institutional resources needed to increase turnout. They canvassed potential voters and urged participation on behalf of party nominees. They conducted "get out the vote" drives, took people whom they expected to vote for the party's candidates to and from the polls, and in general helped maintain in the electorate a sense of partisan awareness and interest. Today, in many areas of the United States, parties do such things less vigorously than they used to.

Who Votes?

People of high socioeconomic status generally vote at a much higher rate than those of low status, data analysis from massive surveys conducted by the Bureau of the Census shows. Education is especially important: it "has a very substantial effect on the probability that one will vote."[9] In 1984, people with college degrees voted at a rate of thirty-six percentage points higher than those with eight years of schooling or less. Income and occupation were much less important as independent factors: once education is held constant, income differences have little effect on rates of voter participation. Yet, the variations of rates of voting by education level are very large within all income groups.[10] Education

> imparts information about politics . . . and about a variety of skills, some of which facilitate political learning. . . . Schooling increases one's capacity for understanding and working

with complex, abstract, and intangible subjects, that is, subjects like politics. . . . Learning about politics doubtless height-
ens interests; the more sense one can make of the political
world, the more likely that one is to pay attention to it.[11]

Presumably, the increasingly complex and abstract character of politics makes education a bigger factor in determining the likelihood of
voting than it was previously. (See Table 2, page 118.)

Partisan Implications

How much do voters differ from nonvoters in political terms? Voters are generally of higher socioeconomic standing and have more
formal education than nonvoters, but are their political interests and
values different? If voters and nonvoters are very different politically,
then the widespread nonvoting in contemporary American politics
means that our electorates can be highly unrepresentative.

As a group, voters used to be slightly higher in Republican identification than the entire adult population by a few percentage points.[12]
This may be changing, however. In 1986, voters were a bit more
Democratic than the voting-age populace as a whole. The main
story is that political differences between voters and nonvoters are
small. "On some issues voters are a shade more liberal than the
entire population; and on others they are a trifle more conservative.
. . . In short, on these issues voters are virtually a carbon copy of the
citizen population. Those most likely to be underrepresented are
people who lack opinions."[13] The tiny difference between voters
and the entire citizenry on various policy issues "suggests that on
these political questions people who vote are representative of the
population as a whole."[14]

Other Forms of Political Participation

Americans may turn out at the polls at a lower rate than their counterparts in other democracies, but they exercise their control over the
political process through a much more extensive array of elections
than any other citizenry. Over 500,000 offices are filled by election
in the United States within every four-year election cycle. "No country can approach the United States in the frequency and variety of
elections and thus in the amount of electoral participation in which
its citizens have a right."[15] No other country chooses the lower
house of its national legislature as often as every two years, as the
United States does. No other country has such a broad array of
offices — including judges, sheriffs, city treasurers, attorneys general
— subject to election. No other country (with the exception of

Switzerland) approaches the United States in the number or variety of local referenda on policy issues. The United States is almost alone in using primary elections as the vehicle for choosing party nominees; in most democratic nations, party organizations pick the nominees. Ivor Crewe concludes that "the average American is entitled to do far more electing — probably by a factor of three or four — than the citizenry of any other democracy."

This suggests a critical modification of the common observation that voter participation is low in the United States. *Turnout* in national elections is indeed low, but in other regards voter *participation* is very high. The American electorate expresses itself in more political decisions through casting ballots than the electorate of any other country.

TABLE 1

Turnout of Registered Voters
National Elections, 1945-80

		Vote as a percentage of registered voters	Compulsion penalties	Automatic registration
1.	Belgium	94.6	Yes	Yes
2.	Australia	94.5	Yes	No
3.	Austria	91.6	No (some)	Yes
4.	Sweden	90.7	No	Yes
5.	Italy	90.4	Yes	Yes
6.	Iceland	89.3	n.a.	n.a.
7.	New Zealand	89.0	No (some)	No
8.	Luxembourg	88.9	n.a.	n.a.
9.	W. Germany	88.6	No	Yes
10.	Netherlands	87.0	No	Yes
11.	United States	86.8	No	No
12.	France	85.9	No (some)	No
13.	Portugal	84.2	n.a.	n.a.
14.	Denmark	83.2	No	Yes
15.	Norway	82.0	No	Yes
16.	Greece	78.6	Yes	Yes
17.	Israel	78.5	No	Yes
18.	United Kingdom	76.3	No	Yes
19.	Japan	74.5	No	Yes
20.	Canada	69.3	No	Yes
21.	Spain	68.1	Yes	Yes
22.	Finland	64.3	No	Yes
23.	Ireland	62.2	No	Yes
24.	Switzerland	48.3	No (some)	Yes

"Compulsion penalties" refers to whether or not the law in each country provides for penalties (fines, etc.) for not voting.

SOURCE: David Glass, Peverill Squire, and Raymond Wolfinger, "Voter Turnout: An International Comparison," *Public Opinion,* December/January 1984, 52. The authors based this table on the most recent national election held in each country as of 1981.

TABLE 2

Reported Voting Rates in
1984 of Selected Groups

Characteristics	Persons of voting age	Percentage reporting they voted
TOTAL	170,000	59.9
Male	80,300	59.0
Female	89,600	60.8
White	146,800	61.4
Black	18,400	55.8
18-20 years old	11,200	36.7
21-24 years old	16,700	43.5
25-34 years old	40,300	54.5
35-44 years old	30,700	63.5
45-64 years old	44,300	69.8
65 years old and over	26,700	67.7
North and West residence	112,400	61.6
South residence	57,600	56.8
Years of school completed:		
8 years or less	20,600	42.9
9-11 years	22,100	44.4
12 years	67,800	58.7
More than 12 years	59,500	67.5*
		79.1**
Employed	104,200	61.6
Unemployed	7,400	44.0
Not in labor force	58,400	58.9

*One to three years of college.
**Four years or more of college.

SOURCE: Nelson W. Posby and Aaron Wildavsky, *Presidential Elections: Contemporary Strategies of American Electoral Politics,* 7th ed. (New York: Macmillan, 1988), based on data from U.S. Bureau of the Census, *Current Population Reports,* series p-20. nos. 192, 253, 359, and 405. From *Statistical Abstract,* 1974, 437; 1977, 491; 1981, 499; 1986, 256.

NOTES

1. Curtis Gans, "The Cause: The Empty Voting Booths, " *Washington Monthly* 10 (October 1978): 28.

2. See Raymond E. Wolfinger and Steven J. Rosenstone, *Who Votes?* (New Haven, Ct., 1980).

3. Howard L. Reiter, "Why Is Turnout Down?" *Public Opinion Quarterly* 43 (Fall 1979): 310. See, too, Reiter, *Parties and Elections in Corporate America* (New York, 1987), 134-57.

4. Frances Fox Piven and Richard Cloward, *Why Americans Don't Vote* (New York, 1988).

5. Ruy A. Teixeira, "Will the Real Nonvoter Please Stand Up?" *Public Opinion* 11 (July/August 1988): 42, 44. See, too, Teixeira, *Why Americans Don't Vote: Turnout Decline in the United States, 1960-84* (Westport, Ct., 1987).

6. Ivor Crewe, "Electoral Participation," in David Butler, Howard R. Penniman, and Austin Ranney, eds., *Democracy at the Polls: A Comparative Study of Competitive National Elections* (Washington, D.C., 1981), 232.

7. Seymour Martin Lipset, *Political Man* (Garden City, NY, 1960), 181.

8. These data have been published in *Historical Statistics of the United States: Colonial Times to 1970,* part 2, 1071-72.

9. Wolfinger and Rosenstone, *Who Votes?*.

10. Ibid., 23-28.

11. Ibid., 18.

12. Ibid., 109-10.

13. Ibid., 109.

14. Ibid., 111.

15. Crewe, "Electoral Participation," *Democracy at the Polls,* 232.

SUGGESTED READINGS

Butler, David. Howard R. Penniman, and Austin Ranney, eds. *Democracy and the Polls: A Comparative Study of Competitive National Elections.* Washington, D.C.: American Enterprise Institute for Public Policy Research, 1981.

Lipset, Seymour Martin. *Political Man: The Social Bases of Politics.* Baltimore, Md.: The Johns Hopkins University Press, 1981. See especially chap. 6.

Piven, Frances Fox and Cloward, Richard. *Why Americans Don't Vote.* New York: Pantheon, 1988.

Polsby, Nelson W. and Aaron Wildavsky. *Presidential Elections: Strategies of American Electoral Politics.* 7th edition. New York: Scribners, 1988. See especially chap. 5.

Teixeira, Ruy A. *Why Americans Don't Vote: Turnout Decline in the United States, 1960-84.* Westport, Ct.: Greenwood Press, 1987.

Wolfinger, Raymond E. and Steven J. Rosenstone. *Who Votes?* New Haven, Ct.: Yale University Press, 1980.

About the Authors

CHRISTOPHER COLLIER is Professor of History at the University of Connecticut at Storrs, a member of the Connecticut Historical Commission, and since 1985, the official Connecticut State Historian. He has published and spoken widely about colonial Connecticut and about the American Revolution. He is author of *Roger Sherman's Connecticut: Yankees, Politics and the American Revolution* (1971) and *Decision at Philadelphia: the Constitutional Convention* (1987).

SEAN WILENTZ is Associate Professor of History at Princeton University. He has published numerous articles on the origins of the American working class and working class culture. His pathbreaking book, *Chants Democratic: New York City and the Rise of the American Working Class, 1788-1850* (1984), won the Frederick Jackson Turner Prize of the Organization of American History and the annual book award of the Society of the History of the Early Republic.

PAUL KLEPPNER is Professor of History and Political Science, and Director of the Social Science Research Institute at Northern Illinois University. Throughout his prolific scholarly career, he has concentrated on the relationship between race, ethnicity and politics. His first book, *The Cross of Culture: A Social Analysis of Midwestern Politics, 1850-1900* (1970), was a pioneering study of religion's and ethnicity's impact on late-nineteenth-century voting patterns. His later works, such as *Who Voted? The Dynamics of Electoral Turnout, 1870-1980* (1982) and *Chicago Divided: The Making of a Black Mayor* (1985), also explored those themes.

ERIC FONER is DeWitt Clinton Professor of History at Columbia University. He has authored numerous books of pathbreaking quality about the political ideology of the American Revolution and the Civil War, especially *Tom Paine and Revolutionary America* (1976) and *Free Soil, Free Labor, Free Men: The Ideology of the Republican Party Before the Civil War* (1970). His most recent book, *Reconstruction: America's Unfinished Revolution, 1863-1877* (1988), which scholars consider the definitive modern treatment of the post-Civil War years, won the 1989 Bancroft Prize in American History.

ELLEN CAROL DUBOIS is Professor of History at UCLA and one of the leading scholars in the field of nineteenth-century women's rights. Her many books and articles have examined nineteenth-century women's rights leadership, female sexuality in the 1800s, and ties between class relations and the nineteenth-century women's movement. She has authored *Feminism and Suffrage: The Emergence of an Independent Women's Movement in America, 1848-1869* (1978) and has edited *Elizabeth Cady Stanton, Susan B. Anthony: Correspondence, Writings, Speeches* (1981). She is currently working on a biography of the turn-of-the-century suffragist Harriet Stanton Blatch.

MARY FAINSOD KATZENSTEIN is Associate Professor of Government at Cornell University. While she began her scholarly career by studying politics and ethnicity in India, she has recently turned her attention to comparative feminist studies, examining women's movements in different countries, and to the study of feminism in the United States. She co-edited the book *The Women's Movements of the United States and Western Europe: Consciousness, Political Opportunity and Public Policy* (1987), and she has published articles about the rights of women in family law and about the 1980s feminist movement in the United States.

LINDA FAYE WILLIAMS, an associate director of research at the Joint Center for Political Studies in Washington D.C., is currently a Fellow at the Kennedy School of Government, Harvard University. Having taught political science at Roosevelt, Chicago State and Howard universities, she has written widely about the role of race in politics, especially in her book, *Race, Class and Politics: The Impact of the American Political Economy on Detroit's Blacks* (1985), and in her numerous articles about black electoral participation, urban politics, and affirmative action.

EVERETT CARLL LADD is Director of the Institute for Social Inquiry and Professor of Political Science at the University of Connecticut at Storrs. He has built a national reputation as a public opinion researcher, and his public opinion polls are cited regularly in major national newspapers. He has published nearly a dozen books on American politics, including his widely used textbook *The American Polity: The People and Their Government* (1989), and his recent book *Where Have All the Voters Gone? The Fracturing of America's Political Parties* (1982).

DONALD W. ROGERS is Assistant Professor of History and Legal Studies at the University of Hartford. Having specialized in American legal and constitutional development, particularly in the fields of regulation and labor law, he is currently at work on a major study of early twentieth-century occupational safety and health administration.